J.F.D.I

JUST F **ING DO IT !

AF226457

J.F.D.I

JUST F **ING DO IT !

A

MANUFACTURING

TURNAROUND

FRANK WALSH

Dedication

*"For my children Daniel & Shona, and their children
Jenna, Lia and Sunny and their children
Dad and Grandad Grumps*

Contents

Forward

Frank Walsh is an enigma and I have known him for over 20 years. He is the best General Manager I have known, but more – Frank can, and has, turned around companies that many considered basket cases, and he does so bottom-up. He actually gets the dysfunctional managers and workers that created the mess to execute the turnaround. But even that is not enough. Frank makes these changes very quickly and most of the workers have nothing but praise for him afterwards.

When I read the book, although fictional, I knew each of the companies he had based the experiences on and there is no exaggeration. Frank is a people person with an uncanny sense of humour. He uses humour as a tool to explain problems and resolve difficult situations. Frank is a very caring person who stands up for the underdog, but he also has a steely streak when he discovers, bullying, dishonesty and oppressive behaviour.

I have told Frank many times that he is more than an Interim Manager. He is the best trouble-shooter to fix dysfunctional companies in the UK. He is the Red Adair of the business world, brought in during a crisis to put out the fires and fix the damage.

This is his first book and should be read by all business managers to inspire and guide them to success. I wish Frank every success.

Joe Booth, access2growth Ltd. October 2018

I've had the pleasure of working for, and with Frank over the last five years. The first time I met him I was struggling to get my improvement plan across to a disengaged audience. With Frank in the room, everyone sat up and took notice. He captured the audience and told it as it was.

That same evening, we went out for dinner and I can honestly say he has been my mentor, and, I'm proud to add, my friend, ever since. Frank is a genuine leader; he is able to motivate both the lop level (the "grown-ups") and the shop floor operatives.

Emma Burnett. Process Improvement Consultant. October 2018

CHAPTER 1

As I sit with a glass of chilled white wine watching the world go by in the airport lounge, relaxing already and reflecting on a job well done, the mobile rings. *"Caller withheld."* I answer it; the voice isn't one I recognize and yet I already know instinctively how this will play out.

The formal sounding voice asked 'is that Frank Walsh?' and I confirm. He introduces himself as a head -hunter specializing in plastics and packaging.

'I got your name from a mutual colleague, is it OK to talk now?'

'Sure', I said.

'I have a company in a bit of bother, and was wondering if you could help. You come highly recommended and your references are first class.'

'What's the bother?' I asked, taking a sip from my glass, watching the rain sprinkling the window, the plane coming in to land, all plans for the holiday momentarily forgotten as I listen carefully.

'Well, they implemented a new ERP system quite badly and everything has gone to pot.'

My wine suddenly tastes bitter; ERP is not the magic bullet they all thought and wished for. 'Anyway, they're two months into their fiscal and declared to the owners that they're going to lose between £2 and 5 million if this continues. Between you and me, I think the writing is on the wall if they do not turn this one around.'

'What's their fiscal? Calendar or tax year?'

'Calendar I'm afraid, and it's already March. They declared a £720k loss for February, and January wasn't much better.'

'So, they've got ten months to turn it around? Who are the owners?' I asked, intrigued, solutions growing in my head as the story unfolded. My magic bullet is one of tested success but it relies on commitment in people and equipment.

'Venture capitalists, Americans I'm afraid, and they certainly want their return on investment.' 'However, I am told they are prepared to stick it out if they can be convinced of a turnaround within the fiscal year and firm foundations are laid for the coming years.'

'Are they prepared to invest?' The magic bullet requires some significant investment in the right areas to be pulled back and put back properly.

'Yes, they've got a lot at stake here. Prestigious plastic manufacturers and high street retailers. If it doesn't perform it will have an impact on their global business and will have a devastating effect on the overall UK business worth £200 million, not to mention their reputation.'

'Yes, I see, you cannot put a cost on poor reputation in the market place.'

'Exactly! Can you help?'

'Certainly, worth a look. What's the package they are offering?'

'Your usual day rate plus all reasonable expenses, such as accommodation and mileage.'

My wine glass is empty, I stare into the glass as I listen to the recruiter. It certainly sounds like an interesting challenge. 'Ok, I have just finished my last assignment and was hoping to have a bit of a break to be honest.'

My flight to Thailand and a 5* luxury holiday is an hour away, I need this break, the reward for my hard work.

'Perfectly understand Frank! However, this is a large plant. Employing 220 people with a £35 million turnover. Due to the nature of the business it's the only real employer in the small town where they are located.'

'I see!' I paused - he's good I will give him that. I feel that spark of excitement in the pit of my stomach. Employment is important to our economy and to those hard-working people who are trying their best to do a good job despite the irresponsible actions of the stakeholders.

I think for a second and continue;

'Let's talk to the interested parties. Could you set up a meeting?'

'How about a week tomorrow - say 11?' they're very keen.'

I will be returning to the UK the day before, jetlagged and tired but this was just the opportunity I was looking for.

'So, I see. Where are they based?'

'I will send you the details; shall l go ahead and arrange it, Frank?'

'Sure, OK.'

'I will take the usual commission?'

'Yes, alright then.'

'Smashing!'

The phone call ends and I sit back and reflect on the challenge that lay ahead.

'Here we go again Frank,' I say to myself with a wry smile as I stand up to board my plane, I know my week of holiday will be taken up with thoughts of this ERP mess.

CHAPTER 2

First Impressions

Just over a week later and the sun tan is already fading as I drive to the new assignment, excited to see what mess is ahead of me that requires fixing. It is drizzling and I nearly miss the company entrance as the wipers smear rain across my windscreen. The worn sign at the front gate tells me I'm at Company Plastics PLC.

The first thing I noticed as I entered the carpark was that the area was very well laid out with the correct amount of disabled parking within the bays allocated for visitors. However, I couldn't park for the number of cars already taking up the bays. Ten in all. They must have a lot of visitors today, I thought, so I had to park on the road outside the perimeter.

I walked to the reception area and I noticed no signs up to indicate who the visitors here today were. Strange! I thought, so how could the workforce and management even know who these masses of people were on site?

As I turned, I noticed two separate bays away from the main visitor's car park just adjacent to the reception area.

To my dismay the two parking bays had been allocated by initials for what clearly was the senior management. So, no parking bays for the visitors available but space for the senior management. Not the best first impression, I thought. The priorities need to change and quick!

I entered a modern and attractive reception area and was surprised to be greeted by a human being. It seems a rare luxury to have a warm greeting and not a rag of a notice telling you to lift the phone and dial an extension number. It was well lit and airy and she was delightful. I later found out her name was Helen.

'Hi I'm Frank Walsh I'm here to see Andrew Foreman.' She smiled and asked me to sign in.

'Many visitors today?' I quizzed.

'No not really.' She seemed bemused by my apparently random question.

Why is it that so many businesses never think about the visitor's overall experience before letting the senior management egos take over car parking bays? So, whose cars, were they? I could guess already but would find out later.

Reassuringly I was then presented with a four-minute health and safety video after which I had to sign and declare that I understood the parameters I was expected to observe whilst within the building. I then sat awaiting my host.

Andrew was above average height, around six two, and middle aged. He appeared to be aging prematurely and was unsteady on his feet. Whether that was a knee, hip problem or gin problem was unclear.

However, he smiled shook my hand heartily (always a good sign) and ushered me into the boardroom which was adjacent to the reception area. Toilet facilities were also on the ground floor which would, I thought, add to the visitor's first impressions and overall positive experience.

See, I don't always look for the bad!

The boardroom had the usual long table surrounded by ten leather high back chairs. I noticed tea and coffee making facilities; another plus point for the visitor (bearing in mind the visitors would mainly be concerned customers at this point).

Andrew walked around to the opposite side of the table and, with an open file at the ready, sat down. He smiled and opened the conversation to the point.

'So, what have you been told Frank? Call me Andy by the way!' I would never call him Andy for reasons which would become clearer as the weeks progressed.

'Well, I was informed that a new ERP system (Enterprise Resource Planning) had been implemented which didn't go to plan and that as a consequence you're missing orders to the customer base.'

As we know, an ERP system can vary and is not only restricted to larger organizations. Unlike MRP 1 (Material Requirement Planning and MRP 2(Manufacturing Resource Planning) ERP is a single, integrated software platform designed to consolidate information across the entire business – including Finance, Sales, Customer Relationship Management (CRM), Stock and operations enabling businesses. This allows the business to make effective and informed decisions, increase productivity, and grow profitability.

Andrew smiled nervously.

'You've been brought here under false pretentions Frank. You see the ERP system implementation has been an absolute disaster. It's exposed frailties within the whole organization from HR to Production, Finance Account receivables and beyond. These frailties have always been here, but it's now that the water level has been lowered that all the hidden rocks are exposed and I fear it will bring us down.'

'I see; how bad is it do you think?'

Andrew sat back in the chair, he glanced across to the window, staring at the rain drops hitting the glass. It was clear he was affected emotionally by all that had happened. He looked tired and frazzled and even though he was the Chief Operating Officer I could see and sense he was at the end of his tether. OK, I needed to find out what was happening here.

'Can you give me a little background to the implementation, the plant and where the business is now?' I probed to get Andrew out of his melancholy state.

'We turned off the last MRP 2 system (Manufacturing Resource Planning) in April last year. It's all been manual ever since.'

'Last year?' I gasped. 'Then it's been nearly a year?'

'Precisely! We sacked the IT Manager for that decision and have been through the wringer since then. It was like a black hole had just swallowed us all and we were totally and utterly blind. On Time Delivery in Full (OTIF) was the first to drop. Customers went from high 80s before implementation to low 20s post, and that's a guess as we couldn't measure it accurately.'

I sat back fearing the worst. Is it too late? Where is the customer loyalty now?

He continued after a long reflective sigh; 'If it wasn't for Daniel and Mark's dedication and strength we would be in a much worse position.'

'Daniel and Mark?' I enquired.

'Yes, Daniel Lockett ,the supply chain manager, and Mark Winters, the Sales Director. Both stalwarts of the organization; they have kept the business going since the 6th of April. That was the day we went live; known now as the black hole for this business.'

I sat back and observed Andrew as he spoke. There was something about him I did not care for. I couldn't tell what it was yet but I would very much like to meet these two guys and get their views.

Andrew continued, 'Mark's relationship with the customers is exemplary, but not even he can curtail his frustration any longer. We have Production and Planning starting a war on Sales. The lead Sales Manager is Julian and Production believe he's interfering when he tries to change the Planner's priorities, using Mark to override other managers. On reflection we should have got more support into the plant sooner. That's why you're here.'

'And Daniel?' I enquired.

'What a talisman for his people! He looks after the supply chain and customer services. Well, not like there's been much of that lately. From cradle to grave. Order to receipt. (OTR) His only nemesis is Scott Mullen.'

'Scott Mullen?'

'Yes, the Manufacturing Manager. He's dedicated, hardworking and I'd say loyal but what an attitude! Not a team player shall we say. I'm thinking he needs to go; that he is part of the problem.'

'Well, let's just take a step back. Is that born out of frustration, do you think?' I enquired.

'Probably doesn't help himself. I just don't know about him, but he comes across as a total arsehole,' he snarled, and I inwardly winced at his raw aggression towards Scott.

I let him talk some more and he started to relax in my company. I always try to get people to open up a little but it can only be done if you are receptive and listening, not verbose and talking. Remember two ears, one mouth, and use them in that proportion I always find. Listen twice as much as talking. Those who talk too much are hiding behind their own voice. Usually, a lack of self-confidence or worse … denial.

'We had a General Manager who, apart from Mark, everyone reported into. We use a matrix style of management. Are you familiar with that?' he enquired.

Of course, I was. I rolled my eyes inwardly but kept a level expression as I was reluctant to tell him my personal views. In my experience matrix management can work if the dotted line reports are specialist in their own field such as contract law, employment law, finance and technical support.

Unfortunately, we tend to give reporting lines into many matrix managements structures and we end up wasting a lot of time replicating reports and duplicating emails to satisfy the matrix system and egos. Remember, a horse never wins with two jockeys, let alone four or five!

'Yes, I am familiar working within that structure.' I placated him.

'Dylan the GM, well, he had been here too long, I guess. Never wanted to change and didn't see the problems so we parted company.'

I remained impassive; there're always two sides to a story, I have found.

'So, we are looking for an interim General Manager to steer the ship to a profitable position, until we can find a permanent replacement.'

'I understand. Tell me why do you think the implementation failed?'

I wanted to get an insight into Andrew's viewpoint on the decisions made during the implementation.

'Well!' he pondered. 'Group IT pushed the button. We were hapless bystanders and when it all went terribly wrong, we were left with the problem. The IT Manager walked. You know how it is.'

I do, and I don't. The IT Manager walked? Ten minutes ago, he told me he had been sacked. Too easy to just blame the IT (Information Technology) department. It was clear to me Andrew was part of the decision making and was avoiding the proportionate blame.

Was Andrew part of the solution or part of the problem? Only time would tell.

'Has there been a business review of the implementation? Lessons learnt for the next time?' I asked.

Andrew raised his eyebrows and exhaled air at the same time.

'I can assure you the owners have told us there will never be a next time.'

Quiet, but avoiding answering my question? Have lessons been learnt? The fact that the Venture Capitalists were not prepared to implement or invest in a new ERP system again, didn't allow for an understanding as to why the faults came about and to ensure that they were never repeated.

Andrew continued; 'So, we have 240 people here at the plant. We turn over around £35million sales. It was supposed to be £41 million but customers have since left because of the IT issues.' Again, blaming one aspect of the business but I kept quiet, letting him carry on.

'The Plant is Unionized: Amicus being the protagonists and they're demanding. Too demanding!'

It was interesting that the COO called the Union protagonists and not partners? I have worked with many Unions whose only interest is the welfare of its members and that of the company they work for.

Again, I remained quiet letting Andrew fill in the gaps, understanding what his issues were.

'Funny! Amicus is the name derived from the AEUW and MSF. Old unions brought together to form one. Ironically Amicus is an anagram for I Sac Um.'

Andrew laughed at his wit. I smiled graciously. It was becoming clear where part of the problem was.

'The ebbtide (earnings before income tax depreciation and accruals) is currently running at a negative. Was running around double digit before the IT problems.'

'I see!' That's all I said, prompting and listening as he went on with the story, never thinking of other possible root causes beyond those of his own opinion.

It's amazing when people in high positions love to hear the sound of their own voices as if they think they are the oracles that must be listened to. The best leaders I have ever worked for have the most tremendous patience to listen, evaluate and then comment when all has been conveyed. It's something I have tried to emulate throughout my career. It works!

'The fiscal year is upon us: We have to submit a 2+ 10 forecast to the owners next week. We're already behind and we are forecasting a loss of around £2 million pounds for the site unless we can pull it around.'

'That's a big ask' I commented. '…in 10 months?' A statement and a question.

'We are through the worst now; things are starting to slowly turn.' Andrew reassured himself.

'Good to know,' I said supportively. It's not fair to judge at this stage although my gut told me otherwise.

Andrew paused, this was the time I was either going to get a quick exit with the obligatory "do you have any questions?" or it was going to be a factory tour.

'What size shoes do you take?' Andrew asked.

'Eights' I replied.

'Ok, I will get some safety shoes for you to look around the site if that's OK?' He picked up the phone, speaking to Scott Mullen, the Manufacturing Manager, and a character I would soon get to know well, for good and for bad.

'Sure' I said, 'but I'm already wearing safety shoes.' Always come prepared. A test was passed. Andrew smiled. The factory tour was about to commence.

Scott Mullen was a tall confident character. As he entered the board room his demeanour was of someone who really didn't want to be there. I sensed he felt it an intrusion on his working day. Non-valued added work and simply complying with a directive from the COO rather than conforming. Andrew introduced me, and without making eye contact Scott shook my hand and looked at Andrew.

'Do I give him the five-dollar tour or the fifty cents?' he asked flippantly.

Andrew replied, embarrassment evident in his face 'five dollars if you don't mind.'

I watched this interaction with interest. The tail is wagging the dog here. I donned my PPE (Personal Protective Equipment) and followed a disgruntled Manufacturing Manager out of the boardroom, through reception and out to the carpark.

As I am only 5ft 7inches I only take little strides and Scott was making it clear he did not want to be there with me. Scott was ahead of me by a country mile and speeding up his pace.

I spoke, giving a reason for Scott to turn around and acknowledge me.

'Excuse me Scott? But who owns all the cars in the visitor's bays?' Scott glanced across to identify the cars.

'That's early shift, they get here at 5.30 in the morning when there's no one here. Shift leaves at two.'

Interesting! As a visitor you can only get a parking spot after 2 pm. Scott walked on and opened a gate with his swipe card, waited and held the gate open for me as I caught up. I thanked him and we moved on at a pace.

'What you want to see?' he asked.

'Everything!' I exclaimed.

His eyes rolled and he sighed. 'Come on then!' leading me towards a large outbuilding adjacent to the car park.

We entered the building and once again Scott held the door open as I could not keep up with his long strides. As we entered there was an outer area to wash hands and change into protective garments before entering the production area. A hair net (not that I had any hair to protect) ear plugs and a white disposable gown.

Scott began to scrub his hands at the mandatory wash area. I followed suit and entered the building.

You can always tell when a manufacturing area is performing. The drum beat of the machines the humming of the wheels in motion and the amount of people interreacting and discussing.

I'm afraid none of this was apparent when I entered the room. Of the five large equipment assets only two were running and one of them at a low speed. People were not to be seen and, as we walked, it was clear there was no supervisory presence on the floor at all.

As we passed the notice boards I stopped and looked. Scott carried on walking. What I found on the boards was that all the key performance indicators (KPI) such as yield, output and downtime were out of date. The boards themselves did not have any titles to describe what they were and the graphs and action reports were all unkempt and dirty.

Scott returned to me after realizing I was actively looking at the boards.

'Don't bother with them - they're a waste of time' he exclaimed.

'Why?' I asked. The first why.

'Because they're meaningless,' he said.

'Why are they meaningless?' I asked. The second why.

'Because all the data is wrong,' he explained.

'Why is all the data wrong?' The third why.

'Because we have no one to fill in all the reporting sheets,' he spoke.

I paused for a second. Scott was getting very agitated with me.

'Why do you not have anyone to fill the sheets in?' The fourth why.

'Well to be honest they're all working on the machines, that's why.'

I paused, then asked the fifth and final why.

'Why can they not fill in the data on the sheets when the machines are running?'

Scott was about to retort automatically, but then something happened. I see it often, and I recognize the expression. Almost a light bulb went on, just for a moment.

He pondered.

Considered what I had asked.

His demeanour turned to a submissive stance. He then looked at me directly and spoke.

'I don't know why they can't, to be fair.' We moved on. This time Scott was walking side by side with me. I didn't know it at the time but Scott would prove a big nut to crack but my greatest ally in the end.

As we entered the next large building, I noticed a glass three-sided enclosed room. I could see people bustling in the area. I quickly realized it was the tea room where operators would go for their breaks. To my astonishment a television set was on, playing football highlights and a scruffy mixture of old sofas and seated chairs adorned the room.

'Can we have a look in there?' I asked.

Scott turned to me. 'Best not at the moment; they're having their break.'

I looked at my watch and, realizing the time, I noted the tea room for another day and moved on with Scott.

Once again, the shop floor was quiet, machinery hummed in the background but the atmosphere was more library than production. Not surprising with the amount of people in the tea room I thought. The display boards were again out of date and untidy.

The visual displays in any work area reflect how that area is run. A porthole into the operation if you like. If the display boards are out of date, untidy and not cared for - well, invariably that's how the area is, also. It certainly was the case here.

Before long we were back in the boardroom where Andrew was pacing up and down with his mobile stuck to his ear. I thanked Scott for his time and he left quickly. I sat down rapidly scribbling some notes on my observations. Andrew finished his call and sat down.

'So, what did you think?' he asked.

'Well.' I paused. 'There's plenty to go at.'

'Such as?' Andrew inquired.

'Housekeeping, visual management, productivity, machine maintenance; there doesn't seem to be a buzz about the place.'

'Buzz?'

'Yes, usually a productive operation has a buzz about it. The constant rhythm of productive machines, the chatting of people being engaged and involved.' I paused to see his reaction. No one wants to tell a parent that their child is ugly, right?

'I see.' Clearly, he didn't. I could tell he was never on the shop floor to feel it, see it and know it. He had no idea what I was talking about.

'You come highly recommended.'

'Thank you,' I said modestly. Andrew picked up my CV from his note pad.

'Says here in your previous assignment that you helped turn around a first-tier supplier to the automotive sector?'

'Yes. It was a three-month assignment that lasted eleven.'

'How did you manage that? Automotive is a tough environment to work in.'

'Certainly is!' I sat upright, cleared my throat and started to reel off the story.

'The supplier had chosen a path with a new technology; one which they were not familiar with. As plastic moulded injectors they were good at what they did, but they wanted more from the process. This was dry-coated paint spray which they were also very familiar with.'

'I see.' Andrew pondered.

'For some reason they decided to go down the electrostatic paint booth route. These charge the jigs holding the component parts and then the paint sticks to them using the electrostatic process. This they were not good at.'

I continued, 'The introduction of new technology was, on paper, a good idea. Cost saving by bringing a costly process in-house and ultimately driven by the high standards of quality from the automotive customers. Unfortunately, the level of investment neglected the amount of skilled personnel required and the amount of training.

I was drafted in to look at the offending paint line. The RTF (Right First Time) was 33% with high levels of scrap and rejection.'

'Wow that's high! I don't feel so bad now.' Andrew smiled.

'Well, it was a tough assignment. I evaluated the situation and within the week my proposal was three-fold. First; I suggested they bring in the technical experience needed to look after a technology that no one had any clue how to operate correctly. Two; form a kaizen event with both the suppliers and the customers.'

'Customers? That's brave!' Andrew challenged, and for the first time the flicker of instinct told me he knew little of my work, or his factory.

'Not really. The customer knew we were failing and they were camped in the plant for months. They took up board rooms and offices, not to mention the car park and all just sat around, arguing and waiting for us to do something differently. They called it suppler support engineers.'

'Were they much help?' enquired Andrew, surprisingly animated as though this was a good idea which it most definitely was not. Who wants their dirty washing airing to their own customer?

'Not really, as they didn't know what to do either. It took all my valuable resources and caused more stress.'

'Ok, I see that. The third thing?' Andrew asked.

'Review the ERP system. It's easy to blame the system, but actually it's the inputs you need to review, not always the way the system is made. We found many hidden flaws in the process which we needed to fix.'

No comment from Andrew on this, so I continued.

'Also, and as an independent consultant who is hands on it was a tough call for me but I insisted that I did not interface with the end customer. By this I meant our automotive client and the owners of the business, or as I call them the grownups.'

'Wow! That couldn't have been easy to sell.' Andrew said.

'Well, the insatiable appetite these automotive supplier support engineers have for meetings and detail was usurping everyone's time. They were hardly out of one meeting before they were summoned to another to explain why they hadn't completed the task raised at the previous meeting. It was counterproductive.'

I continued. 'Then there were the owners of the plant.'

'The grownups,' smiled Andrew.

'Yes. They almost wanted the same amount of reassurance and attention as the customer wanted. It was impossible to actually get anything done. So, I turned it around psychologically, threw it into the arena and arranged a kaizen event. This meant the supplier engineers were on board getting results and they would ultimately become part of the solution and not the hindrance they were being. This had two effects: they were being utilized, and felt they were actually contributing and could also funnel back to the seniors how things were getting done.'

'I see. Smart!' Andrew acknowledged.

'The third thing was to look at the inventory control. Apparently, according to the data we had capacity for the business and yet we had loads of stock. However, we were still failing the customer and as we discovered, it was not only on the product that went through the electrostatic paint line, but everywhere else.' I paused for effect, waiting for the penny to drop. Andrew nodded. 'So, we were playing all the right notes but not necessarily in the right order!'

'The recruitment of experienced personnel also included a new top layer of management from the automotive sector.'

'A whole new layer?' exclaimed Andrew.

'Yes, the business had won major contracts from an exceptional sales force; however the operations didn't keep up. People and processes were not invested in and the new paint line just exposed all that.'

'Big problems then.'

'Oh yes! We were airlifting component parts via helicopter to the automotive plants as we were stopping the lines.'

'Really?'

'Yes. When I got there, seeing all those helicopters lifting off from the car park, it looked like a scene from Apocalypse now!' Andrew laughed.

"So, I set about the three-pronged attack with the recruitment, the kaizen, and the proper implementation and investigation into the ERP system.'

'How did it go?' Andrew enquired.

'Well, the kaizen event moved the RFT (right first time) from 33% to 70% in four weeks.'

'Wow! Impressive.'

'Yes, this then highlighted the downstream problem. The moulding machines couldn't keep up with the paint line. Always creates another bottleneck elsewhere in the system when you fix one part.' Andrew nodded, listening intently. 'In parallel to this, I set up the ERP system crew to look at the bills of material pricing and routes. Typically, these hadn't been looked at in years so a fresh look at them showed we were running unnecessary quantities through the business due to the reorder levels set in the system. MOQ (minimum order quantities) were too high. This was driven by the wrong KPI. OEE not OTIF. We changed that quickly. It meant more tool changes, from 30 a week to 20 a day.'

I paused and continued, 'this produced the right amount of component parts; ones which the customer actually required.'

'The recruitment went really well. We paid top rates to a high quality outside recruitment agency but got a quick and positive response.' I paused again.

'Expensive recruiters?' Andrew declared, a flicker of concern on his face.

'Yes they are, but if you think hiring professionals is too expensive for your business, try hiring amateurs! Look Andrew, within three months we had stopped the helicopters and the stoppages at the customer plants. We had then moved from 70% RFT on the paint line to 98% RFT.'

'We managed to get good solid people from the automotive industry to work with us. Automotive shall speak unto automotive! So, we were removed from a high status of dependency to a low one within the three months. The meeting rooms were emptied and my car park was available again.'

'Wow! That was truly inspirational.'

'Thank you' I replied.

'Can you do the same here?'

'I can't see why not.'

This situation wasn't so far from the previous assignment. A problem statement, no - multiple problem statements - were already forming using my head and my gut this time. I would bet my first month's wages that data would support my instincts, but I kept this to myself. Some cause and effects were easy to spot, from the outside anyway.

Lack of leadership from the top and at middle management level.

No sense of purpose and no momentum within the plant.

Certainly not customer focused.

Once you get this type of rot it filters down the line.

Disengaged employees and an atmosphere of feeling as though they can run amok in the place.

Andrew then went on to describe the culture of the business and the reporting lines into the USA central functions. He then mentioned the customer's dissatisfaction on the lack of improvement and that they were becoming disillusioned with it all. After listening to all the internal political turmoil, I began to summarize.

'So, in summary, we are way behind budget with only ten months of the year in which to claw it back. The customers are descending upon us every day for answers that we cannot give them, and the owners are demanding that we turn this around or they will close the plant.'

'Yes, that's it in a nutshell.'

'Sounds like a challenge' I said, smiling before asking the golden question.

'When would you like me to start?' Andrew leapt to his feet and put out his hand mirroring my smile, a sense of hope in his face. I stood up and we shook.

'Tomorrow?'

CHAPTER 3

The First Day

I nervously entered the board room. I hide my nerves well but the first day is always going to be a challenge, meeting the headliners. All eyes on me. The senior management team awaiting my appearance.

Andrew stood up and greeted me. He turned to the team and announced;

'Ladies and Gentlemen, can I introduce you to Frank Walsh. Frank has joined us as interim General Manager while we find a permanent replacement.' He continued. 'Perhaps we should go round the table; get some introductions made; the usual – name position and time served?

Andrew looked around the room and picked on the first person who caught his eye. 'Can we start with you?' Andrew gestured, no - he actually pointed, to a middle-aged woman with short cropped hair who was clearly a local by her accent. I already found Andrew's direct style a little rude but pushed that thought away for a moment.

'Er… OK, I'm Sarah Collingsworth. I am the Quality Manager. I have been here eighteen months but it's my second time here. I was here for many years before I left to have my family.' She smiled. I nodded in acknowledgement of her. Next.

'Mark Winter, Sales Director and I have been here coming up for two years.' I tried to make a remark to lighten his mood. 'So' I said 'it's all your fault!' He was not amused. Next;

'Hi, I'm Daniel Lockett, I'm the Supply Chain Manager, been here twelve months.' Next:

'Scott Mullen, Production Manager, been here three and a half years.' Interestingly, Scott didn't make eye contact.

'I'm Graham Paul, Engineering Manager, been here too long….' We laughed. '…some might say, but it's 22 years.'

'I'm Paula Bartram, HR manager and I have been here a year.'

'Stuart Carr, Finance Controller, been here three months.'

'Wow!' I exclaimed. 'A fairly new team it seems.' I tuned to Andrew to take over.

'Well, that's the senior leadership team for this site,' he declared.

I nodded and acknowledged all of the managers sitting around the table.

If you are managing a new team, then it is important to meet as soon as possible. Having you as their new manager is a change for them and they will need reassurance that life with you in charge is going to be OK. Having a new manager can be unsettling and acknowledging people's feelings is important if they seem anxious or concerned.

Reassure them that you won't be making any drastic changes, or if that is what you have been asked to do, tell them that there may be some changes.

Emphasis that your key objective is to get to know them and their roles so that you can support them.

Introduce yourself, give the same information that you want them to give to you, such as where you have worked before and what you did. Also give them something that you enjoy doing outside of work. Make yourself human!

'Hi I'm Frank, I live in Hertfordshire so a long distance away. I will be staying overnight during the week. I've got two children, one boy and one girl, 28 and 25. Funny names I know, but we like them.'

The room laughed; humour is a great ice breaker. Be careful though, it needs to be handled delicately. Self-deprecation is always a safe bet.

'As you can hear from my accent, I support Manchester United.' Groans from all round particularly the Yorkshireman, Mark Winters.

'I have worked in many businesses from Automotive, aerospace and print.' I continued. 'Most recently for a glass manufacturer. The largest plant in the UK.' I looked around but they didn't seem too impressed. 'It goes to show, it doesn't matter if you are making sausages or tanks it's the methodology that you apply that makes it all work.'

'Any questions?' Silence. No eye contact from most of the team. Mark, the most senior of them all, spoke up.

'How long are you going to be here? I only ask as you're the third GM I've worked for here and I've only been here two years.'

'As long as it takes,' I replied. It was clear that this relatively new team had been through it. They were tired and fed up it seemed, with no clear direction. Once thing was clear though - they needed leadership and I was determined to give that to them.

'So, tell us how you achieved all this in the past.' Again, from Mark, clearly the spokesmen of the group.

I stood up cleared my throat and began.

'The past isn't important today. What's important is how we are going to fix this plant. So, here's what's going to happen. Firstly, you will each have a one to one with me monthly. It will be fixed in both our diaries. No excuses or reschedules please.

How I establish my credibility to each and every one of you and to my peers....' I turned to Andrew and acknowledged him. '.... during the first three months in my new role will be crucial to our success moving forward.'

I now had the attention of everyone in the room.

'What I tend to do is get some early wins. Do one or two things early on that have needed doing for some time which are important or dramatic, or that lots of people will benefit from. Make an impact!'

'Like what?' interrupted Graeme.

I start my first lesson in how I work.

1. Invest in People first.

'Invest in welfare for people. For instance, refurb the canteen. Refurb toilets, etc. This sends a message that we care and that we are here to stay for the long term. Do not ask of your fellow workers something when you give nothing in return.'

Graeme nodded. 'Well, we could do with a decent canteen.' All agreed! Duly noted!

2. Pick 4 key items to focus on. Complete them well.

'I tend to initiate focus on the most important things. Only do four things - not a log of twenty or so, as with the best intentions in the world you will never complete them all. Just do four things. When those are done completely, then do another four.' The room was gripped.

It isn't just a case of cherry picking though; identify the top 4 result areas and focus on these. Spend time proactively assessing and addressing areas that limit, or could improve, productivity or effectiveness. When the team start to see results. THAT'S when confidence will begin to form.'

I had to shake them out of their dour attitude. I started to walk around the room as they were all seated.

3. Deliver on Commitments.

'It's important to deliver on commitments. I have a mantra - I say what I will do, and I do what I say. Never commit to anything unless you fully understand what it's going to take to achieve it. When you meet every commitment you make, showing that you can get things done then the team will believe in you, they may even start to believe in themselves.

'However, you must keep a balance between competing pressures; this is the ultimate measure of your management and leadership skills.'

4. Be honest about knowledge.

'I never pretend that I know things you don't. I have found you will always be found out. If you don't know, ask or find out. Everyone learns by their mistakes and many of the things we learn that really stick are things we got wrong at the start and had to change.'

5. Stay calm and focused at all times.

'Be confident, relaxed and positive at all times even when things are going wrong. As a leader if you panic everyone panics. The closest I get to panic is picnic.' I got a few smiles from that so I continued, 'Even if sometimes you do feel the pressure just smile and keep on going. Leaders who show stressful characteristics send the wrong messages to their teams.' There was a nervous laugh at that comment.

6. Focus on the positives.

'Keep things in perspective and always focus on the positive – what you have achieved rather than what you haven't. The glass must always be half full, not half empty.'

Negativity breeds negativity so focus on the positives.

7. Keep emotions at bay.

'Manage your emotions. Emotion will evoke emotion. Keeping your emotions in check can be tough but it is essential for long term credibility. Your direct reports, and all the operators, they are anxious, worried and nervous about the future. This means they need to see strong leadership from all of us here in this room.' Many were now starting to nod vigorously at my comments so I continue with my favourite part.

8. Manage Work/life balance.

'Manage work/home balance. Take time out to enjoy your life and relax. How you act now will set people's expectations for the future so start as you mean to go on.

Home life is the most important and I want my staff to go home at night and take time out to recharge.'

9. Have the vision clearly mapped out.

'After a couple of weeks in this role I will have started to formulate a clear vision of what we need to do to move forward. I will base this on the inputs from all of you in this room and other people I will also talk to. Then it will be time to act. We will need to map out where we want to go and see what needs to be done to get there. Once we are clear on our goals and strategy, we need to discuss and agree them with you and your teams.'

I paused.

'Do you know why?' I asked.

Silence.

'We MUST get all the middle managers to buy in. I don't want people on the team who don't believe in the vision we are aiming for. They will become blockers to the improvement plans.'

'Even if you talk to your teams every day you might wish to arrange a special meeting to discuss and agree our plans.'

Communication is key! I will return to that later.

I pour myself a glass of water from the jug on the table, taking a sip before I continue.

10. Structured Project Management.

'Get your teams to buy in. You can only do this when you have acceptance for the plans, then you will need to agree an action plan with your teams. Our aim is to ensure that everyone in your team is clear what you want to achieve, HOW you are going to do it and WHO will be responsible for WHAT.'

'Team Based Project Management works well for me. A milestone and RACI assessment sheet in one Excel document. It's easy to run through weekly updates and spot any blockers or failures immediately.'

I stop talking and make eye contact around the room. Faces are alert and interested, apart from Scott, who is biting his lip, disinterested and staring out of the window. Purposefully closing himself down and on the defensive. I ignore him and continue to throw soundbites around the room. I will refer back to these often, my golden rules - reinforcing behaviours I expect from a senior management team.

11. Set Measures for success.

'Show me how I am measured and I will show you how I perform.' This is why I love and hate KPI's. I find them limiting and they can drive shortcuts to get jobs done. I do however need them for our benchmark reporting.

12. Internal communication and marketing the changes. Also known as Change Management!!

'Finally, make sure you do a really good job of internal marketing. Communicate to everyone who is affected. We don't want to create the secret society of people in the know alienating useful team members and creating Chinese whispers.'

I sat down in silence. The team looked at each other slightly stunned. I broke the silence.

'That's how I do it.'

It was clear to me that this team had a long way to go and I was looking forward to spending time with them, finding out who they were and what personality type I was dealing with. At every new assignment I always tell the story of the Tortoise, the Rabbit and the Fox. It's an interesting yarn but works quite well. It gets people thinking about what kind of personality type they identify with.

In my experience there's three types of managers within an organization. I relate to the animal kingdom when assessing my managers.

First style is the tortoise. A loyal, hardworking member of the team who only goes at their pace. If you probe them to go faster, they just recoil back into their shells. If you allow them to get to the finishing line at their own pace they will get there.

Second style is the rabbit. A loyal, hardworking member of the team with so much energy and drive that they run off in one direction completing only 80% before they change direction and start another path. You must harness this energy and passion and control them.

The third is the fox. This is not a loyal hardworking member of the team. This manager will say all the right things, look as though they are doing the right things, but have their own hidden agenda. The problem is foxes frighten the rabbits and the tortoises.

If you ask a farmer what happens when he shoots the local fox? - More rabbits come out of their burrows and more tortoises come out of their shells!

I tell this story to my new team and, when I finished the analogy, it was met with some smiles and approving nods from some of the managers. It was Scott, however, who broke the silence first.

'So, Frank what style are you then? A tortoise, rabbit or a fox?'

I replied immediately, not missing a beat. 'I'm a fox hunter!'

USEFUL NOTES:

Below is a list of questions that you may wish to ask a team member at a first one to one meeting. You might want to give each person an outline of the questions below so they can prepare beforehand:

How long have you been working here?
What is your current role and responsibilities?
What did you do before joining here?
What are your current objectives?
What do you enjoy most about your role?
What do you enjoy least about your role?
What do you think you do best?
What do you think you could do better?
What is your key challenge?
What do you feel could be improved in the team?
What motivates you?
What de-motivates you?

What training do you think you would benefit from?
What are your long-term goals?
What is important to you at work?
How do you like to be rewarded?
What are you looking for from a manager?

CHAPTER 4

The Tip of the Iceberg

With the introduction finished I went about organizing the one-to-ones with each of the team members.

When I do this, I make sure that I go to their offices and their domains. I shadow them for an hour to understand the day-to-day structure, and more importantly, how they interact with their direct reports and the operators. Don't bring them over to your office - which is far from a level playing field - you will not get the inside track on what they are all about. This is pivotal to gain their trust and support going forward.

When trying to gauge the company DNA it's important to create a Strategy Driver. This is a valuable resource tool to target the needs of the people within the business. It consists of four questions and then the answers are compiled under the heading that shows the employees desires and wants.

The four questions ae as follows.

1. What is it you do here?
2. How long have you worked here?

3. If there was one thing you could change to improve the overall business what would it be?
4. If there was one thing you could change to improve your department what would it be?

This is a time-consuming element but important to gauge the barometer of feeling within the business. This highlights morale and the real issues the people are facing. Once analysed you make very quick wins in eliminating the top issues by addressing them, which forms the 'strategy driver' document.

Here are some actual examples from three very different businesses and industries. As you can see the second question answers total the length of combined service within the business. How as an organization would you (or should) ignore 100 years + service. Sad to say when the Directors are confronted with these inconvenient home truths, they ignore it. These are the companies that no longer exist.

21 Personnel in 5 departments with a combined service of 310 years were asked 4 Questions :

1. What is it you do here.
2. How long have you been here.
3. If there was 1 thing you could change to help the overall business what would it be.
4. If there was 1 thing you could change to help your department what would it be.

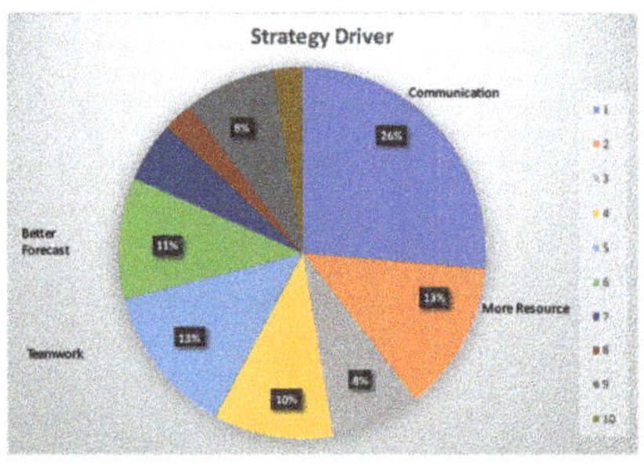

This Drives the Next Steps.

26 Personnel in 3 sites over 6 departments with a combined service of **127 years** were asked 4 Questions :

1. What is it you do here.

2. How long have you been here.

3. If there was **1** thing you could change to help the overall business what would it be.

4. If there was **1** thing you could change to help your department what would it be.

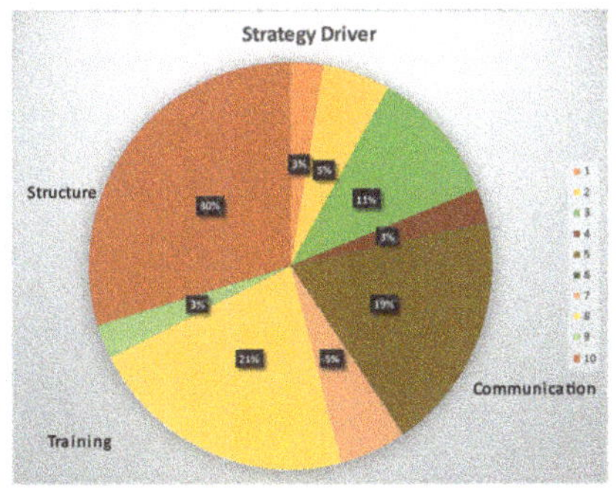

This Drives the Next Steps.

Now from the valuable contribution made from the employees develop your strategy to address their issues. In my experience its communication and teamwork that is lacking. Daily Management Systems and Training address these important problems. These are addressed in the following chapters.

The first one-to-one is always with your internal customer. In this case, the seasoned professional Sales Director, Mark Winters. Mark was a tall, slim man, his short dark hair showing flecks of grey. He was immaculately dressed, clearly highly motivated and outspoken in his arena. The only thing we had in common when we first met was that we were the same age.

Mark had been with the business six months before the black April of the ERP switch on. In that time, he'd managed to grow the sales using his influential skillset and charm. Mark was very outspoken about the lack of product being generated and didn't mind who he told. Including the business owners – 'the grown-ups!'

One of the hardest jobs in any manufacturing organization is Sales. I have total empathy for the external Sales people who are constantly on the road plying for business in difficult market conditions. Compounded by the lack of service from Operations it can be soul destroying, firefighting issues instead of growing business. When you firefight for any length of time you end up being burnt out.

Imagine how difficult is it to go to an unsatisfied customer who once again has not received his/her order to ask for new orders? This is stretching the relationship and friendship a little too far. Really, it's no wonder Mark felt aggrieved and let down by manufacturing.

'So then, you're going to get us out of this mess, are you?' Mark asked as he shook my hand.

'Yes, with your help we can.'

'It's a bloody mess. Not sure how long I can keep my team on board and motivated.'

'Who's on your team?' I asked, trying to diffuse the moment. Remember two ears one mouth.

'Well, I've got Julian and Tim, key account managers for the biggest two customers. Rachel is our Internal Sales Administrator; she's an absolute diamond. We've also got Sanjay and Phil who are Area Sales Managers and we are also recruiting one more for the industrial markets.'

'Yes, I've heard of Julian; he's causing a little disruption with the planning?'

'Rightly so if you ask me! The factory is not producing the right amounts of the correct products and his customers are screaming.'

'Yes, but it doesn't help when he demands the plan to change just for his clients. It disrupts the whole business. More set-up, more downtime and it's a spiral we cannot get out of.'

'Well, we need the product. Simple as that.' Mark retorted. I backed off as this was beginning to become a confrontation not an initial meet and greet.

'Anyway, good to meet you but I'm afraid I'm going to have to get on a weekly progress call with one of our biggest accounts. The weekly bollicking with no answers and certainly no support from operations.'

'Really? Why aren't operations on the call with you in support?'

'They never turn up. We're left with the sharp end.'

'Where's Scott in all this?'

Marks's demeanour changed again.

'Don't talk to me about Scott. He's a nightmare!' Mark scurried off to his dreaded phone conference call.

After meeting and greeting your internal customer the next step is to go to the department which holds all the answers. Planning. All Material Planning and Logistics fell under the remit of the ever-youthful looking Daniel Lockett, the supply chain manager. I went off to find him but as I looked around at the flurry of disorganized panic, I reminded myself of the "Iceberg of Ignorance" as I refer to it.

With the iceberg only 4% is showing on the surface. This represents the problems the external executive team see. The senior management are paddling in the water with 6%. Middle management are swimming and see 20% of the problems. However, the workforce, they have the full scuba kit on, they see 80% of the problems! They know the answers but only if you can persuade them to give them to you. Just in case those mathematicians amongst you perceive the obvious error - this sum adds up to 110%. That's because middle management share some of the operator's issues and understand the same problems.

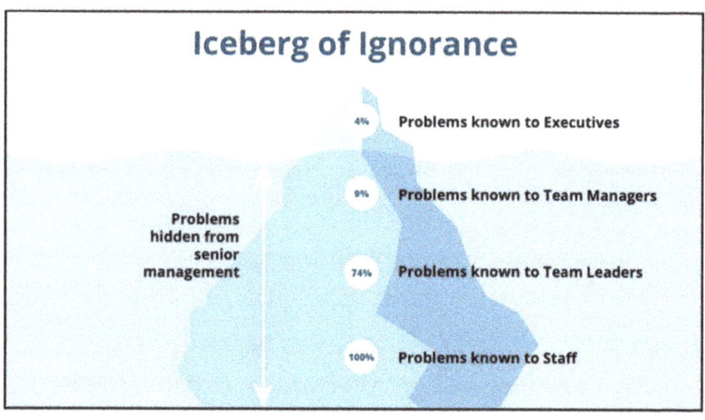

I waited a while in the Customer Services and Planning Office seemingly invisible to those around me. Eventually I was spotted.

'Who are you looking for, mate?' I turned to see a rather scruffy, overweight, long-haired man. 'You look lost, wandered off from the street, have you?'

'Daniel? I am looking for Daniel.' I paused for effect. … 'And I'm not your mate; I am the new General Manager of this plant.' He reeled back embarrassed.

'Sorry, Daniel just popped out. He'll be back soon.'

It's important to set boundaries. This employee didn't know who I was. For all he knew I could have been a disgruntled customer or, worse for him, his bosses' boss!

I returned to my office which by now I had made sparse and had thrown out all of the unwanted papers and books which had been lying around. My desk contained only a screen and keyboard.

My white boards were totally bare. The office looked abandoned. I always start with my office like this because when I roll out the 5S campaign I need to lead by example.

Daniel bowled in, as always positive and smiling. He reminded me of Keith Chegwin on speed!

'I heard you were looking for me?'

'Yes, Daniel I was. Sit down would you, please?'

Daniel sat at the round meeting table in the corner of my office. I then sat opposite him rejecting the big black leather chair behind my desk. I find a desk between work colleagues is a barrier and will always sit with them at the same table.

'Daniel. Can you tell me a little about yourself?' I sat back and listened as Daniel then proceeded to give me a full history of his working career to date. He basically came from a logistics and planning background, working with one of the top five supermarket chains in the supply chain and, it seemed, covered a vast area of the country. Daniel was engaging and pleasant, also very knowledgeable. When he finished, I simply asked him a question?

'So, what do you think is going wrong here?' His smile disappeared but only for a second.

'Well, where do I start? The ERP system implementation was a nightmare and we have been hand to mouth ever since, and the customers are not happy. Morale is low and we need to get out of this slump. People are worried about their future, as am I.'

'Andrew tells me the owners are very supportive and are investing over £750k in new equipment?' I probe, seeing how much Daniel knows.

'Yes, can't get here quick enough,' Daniel retorted.

'If there's one thing we could do to help you and your team what would it be?' I asked.

Daniel thought for a second. 'I guess, better communication between us, and them in Operations.' Interesting the words US and THEM.

'What's the communication like between you and Scott then?'

'Not good,' Daniel said immediately.

'Have you tried?' I asked.

'Yes, in the early days, but Scott is so busy running around trying to fix things it's difficult to get time with him.'

I ponder this for a moment. I have no reason to doubt Mark. I have also had first-hand experience of that. What about the rest of your team?' I enquired.

'They're all great. Really supportive of each other; no wonder, with the amount of abuse they get from the customers.'

'Abuse?'

'Yes, some customers can get rather nasty.'

I paused and leaned over to Daniel to look him straight in the eye.

'Daniel, under no circumstances does anyone have the right to abuse anyone at work, verbally or physically, whether they are the chairman, the COO, CEO or the customer representative.'

Daniel looked surprised at this supportive stance.

I continued,

'We have a duty of care for everyone on this site. The customers have a right to be angry and frustrated but do not have the right to take it out on your staff.'

Daniel sat forward in his seat, listening intently. 'Everyone needs a boss, and they want and need your support. Do not allow anyone under any circumstance to belittle your staff because they have a title that sounds important. Think if it was outside of work in a social event like a pub or a party. Would you let them speak to you like that? So, what gives them the right while you're at a place of work?'

Daniel sat there thoughtfully. I could see he was mulling it over in his mind and was already identifying the individuals within the customer base that were demonstrating these negative behaviours. It was clear Daniel was never supported in dealing with difficult customers.

'So Daniel, who is the most difficult customer representative you are dealing with at the moment?'

Daniel didn't need to think. 'Nick Carter! He is the buyer from one of the biggest accounts. He is unforgiving and bullying.'

'When's the next conference call with this Nick?' I asked. 'Two o'clock today,' Daniel looked at his watch. 'Ok if I sit in on it?'

Daniel, surprised, answered, 'Sure, I would welcome the support.'

'OK, see you at two.' I smile and we stand up together as I close the discussion. Daniel clears his throat and speaks .

'Oh, I understand you had words with James?'

'James?' I enquired. 'Yes, you came in looking for me and he called you mate?'

'Yes, I recall.' 'He didn't mean anything by it you know; it's just his manner. Daft sense of humour but a really good guy.'

'I understand, but he didn't know who I was. I could have been anyone.'

'Yes, but he did know who you were. We all know who you are. He was trying to be friendly and reaching out, not being intimate or disrespectful.'

I like to stop and consider alternative points of view. Just because I am put in a position of corporate authority does not give me the right to assume I am correct. I paused and considered the statement Daniel was making. Sometimes the mentor becomes the mentored. A lesson I learnt myself.

'I'll have a chat with him the next time I see him,' I said. 'Thanks Daniel, see you later at the meeting. '

I put my hand out and he took it, flashing a genuine smile before scurrying off at a pace like a man with a mission.

From that day on I promised myself to mentor Daniel. I saw great potential in him.

CHAPTER 5

The Unions

One of the very first meetings to arrange on your first day in the job is with the representation of the workforce, even if it's not a unionised plant. I have been fortunate to work with all types of unions, mostly good reps though some not so good. This shows clear intent that you value the representative and respect the position they hold, and that the workforce is being listened to and taken seriously.

Always make an early meeting with the Unions or the employee's forum. Reassure them and listen to what they have to say. A few days later I found myself sat at my table with the union representative.

'Hi, I'm Chris McAteer, union rep for the business.' A burly, middle-aged man extended his hand (looked like a bunch of butcher's sausages) for a welcome greeting. We shook hands warmly.

'So, Chris how long have you been here?'

'28 years' man and boy.'

I smiled.

'Well Chris what would you like to discuss? How is the morale on the shop floor?'

His mood changed.

'Well, this total mess the management have made of this plant.' I nodded. 'You're the third GM we've had in as many years.' I continued to nod and not interrupt him. It was clear I was going to get the torrent of his frustration. I decided to brace myself for incoming.

'This is a community factory; most of us have been here all our lives and live in the surrounding areas. If this goes pear shaped there's a lot of people who are going to lose more than their livelihoods. As we see it, the responsibility is due to the total incompetence of senior management. I know we're in trouble, but no one talks to us; no one communicates with us as about what level of trouble we are in. Treated like kids we are, but we're all adults! We have responsibilities, mortgages and we have children of our own. We are adults, so why can we not be treated as such?'

I nod, acknowledging his frustration and he continued,

'We had employee forums which have died off now because we don't go to them, as whatever we ask for, nothing gets done. Waste of our time! No pay rise and no explanation as to why. I've got outstanding bullying and harassment cases to resolve but no one from HR can give me dates. My members are nervous, anxious and thoroughly disappointed. So, Mr Walsh what are you going to do about it?'

He paused and sat back, red faced and angry.

'Well firstly, please call me Frank. Is it OK if I call you Chris?'

Chris nodded in agreement. This technique puts both people on a level playing field as equals.

'I'm sorry that your members feel this way and I can completely understand their frustrations,' I continued. 'It might help if you could indulge me for a moment so I can tell you something about my background.'

Chris grunted arms folded.

'I'm one of five sons to a working-class family. I was bought up on a council estate and I have never gone to university.' Chris looked surprised with my honesty. 'I came from the shop floor and have dealt with incompetent managers all my working life. I found through years of experience that it's usually because the managers haven't been supported or trained, and are expected to do what is a difficult job.'

I continued, 'However that does not excuse bullying and harassment for which I can assure you, Chris, I have zero tolerance.'

Chris's arms unfolded as I spoke, looking him firmly in the eye.

'Well, there's this outstanding case I'd like you to take up immediately.' This was the first challenge and a barometer of what I would do.

'Nadeem, the operator in the warehouse. Nice lad and he's been on suspension now for weeks.'

'Weeks?' I said in disbelief.

'Welcome to the plant Frank. I'd like you to look at this case. Nadeem is worried he's going to lose his job and even though he is being paid, he is not getting the opportunity to work overtime.'

'Chris, I will look at this right away I can assure you.' Chris nodded but continued to tell me of other cases, grievances and issues the workers had. When he ran out of steam he stopped and asked me what I was going to do about the rest of the cases he had to deal with.

'What are you going to do about all these points then, Frank?' Chris leaned forward, waiting for an answer.

'OK. Let's get a list together now, a proper one we can work on. I need time to evaluate it all. I assure you I will get back to you by the end of the week. We need a monthly schedule for employee forums whereby you and the representatives can talk directly to me with HR in tow. I will instigate monthly town hall meetings for all the shifts and will be present at them all. I can assure you that all your concerns will be addressed in a timely manner. After all, it's the workforce that makes the competitive advantage against our competitors. People with ties cost me money - people without ties make me money.' I paused.

Chris smiled, 'Well you got a lot to live up to Frank. I guess we will see.'

'Yes, we will; talk is cheap, actions are what we need.' Chris stood up and held his hand out. We shook warmly and then he left. I knew I could work with Chris because his only concern was not for his empire but for the people he represented. To help and support his fellow workers for such little reward. I picked up the phone to Paula.

'Hi Paula, can I have a copy of Nadeem's files please? Right away.'

Two hours later, after a review of the Nadeem file it was clear that some investigative work was required. I sat back and took a breather, just a minute of quite time and short lived as Scott entered my room, accompanied by Paula.

'Hey Scott thanks for coming.'

Scott sat down with no response. Paula sat beside me.

Never have a conversation which could lead to confrontation without someone, preferably an HR representative, beside you. You could fall into a lot of trouble I have found! Paula was there to observe and take notes.

'I wanted to understand a little more about Nadeem.'

I stood up to close the door, Scott needed to know this was serious.

'Oh him!' Scott announced discouragingly. I sat opposite Scott waiting for more detail.

'Well, he refused a reasonable request from one of my team leaders. It was month end and as usual we were all rushing around to get the stock shifted in the warehouse ready for a load, because as you know, if we don't move fast the drivers would be calling to say we were delaying them again.'

I don't say anything waiting for the story to unfold.

'Well Charlie, the forklift driver, comes hurtling around the corner and as a result his load fell off the forklift. No one hurt thankfully. So, Rob the shift lead asks Nadeem to help pick up the fallen load which was spilling out all over the floor. It was dangerous and he needed Charlie to get back to loading the lorries. Well, Nadeem refused so Rob asked him again and he refused again. Rob came to see me and I suspended Nadeem pending further investigation.'

'How long ago was that?' I asked.

'Two weeks,' came the reply. I looked up in amazement. 'I know. I should have sorted it by now but with all the other things going on….' he tapered off as he saw my expression. I could not hide my disappointment.

'Get Nadeem in here today.' I demanded. 'I want to hear his side of these events that took place.' Scott was visibly shocked. 'Also, where are the statements from Charlie and Rob? They were not in the file.'

'They were verbal statements given' declared Scott.

'Scott, there are so many issues here. I cannot begin to describe the disappointment I am feeling. Go and get written statements from both of them and I want them on my desk before Nadeem comes in this afternoon. This is not a request! Do the job you should have done in the first place!'

Scott blushed angrily and stood up. "I've got twenty-eight years' experience! I'd have you know!"

I retorted. 'Are you sure it's not one year's experience twenty-eight times?'

Scott walked out of the office without saying a word.

Nadeem was a twenty-two-year-old English Asian man, slightly built with a nice smile. He nervously entered my office with Chris his union representative behind him.

'Come in Nadeem, please take a seat.' He sat down nervously looking at Chris for reassurance. Chris nodded reassuringly.

'Nadeem, firstly can I apologise for the delay in seeing you. I'm sure it has been a worrying time.' Nadeem nodded and looked at Chris.

'That's something I will be addressing. The length of suspension is unacceptable.'

'I've heard and read the reported incident and I was wondering if I could have your side of events please?'

Nadeem cleared his throat.

'Well, I was on late shift in the despatch area of the warehouse.'

'Yes', I prompted.

'Charlie comes round the corner with a pallet on. He took the corner too quickly; I guess he was rushing around being month end, an' all.' Nadeem looked at Chris as though to ask if Charlie was in trouble.

Chris patted his shoulder.

'Go on lad, you can tell Frank everything.' This was music to my ears; Chris had the belief that I would listen impartially.

'Well, the load fell over and the components spilled all over the floor. We all looked around and Charlie were getting out of his driver seat when Rob the team lead come up. He told Charlie to get back in his cab and get another load. Rob then turned around to me and clicked his fingers. He shouted "Nadeem clean this up!"'

We all sat in shock. Nadeem continued, he looked down at the floor, not making eye contact, clearly still upset. 'I was embarrassed at being clicked like that with fingers and in front of all my mates. Rob got mad when I didn't do what he wanted and he started shouting, "Did you hear what I said? Pick this mess up?" So, I replied, "I didn't make the mess." It wasn't that I wouldn't have picked up the mess; I would have helped, but it was the way he was talking. He was bang out of order and he got madder, shouting "Don't speak back to me. Just do it." I said no and turned my back and continued to pack. I was shaking at this point, so mad, it was 'cos I felt like he was picking on me 'cos I'm the youngest, and well, you know... Well in about ten minutes Scott came back with Rob. Scott was shouting and all, and I've seen him like that before but not with me. "Nadeem is that right you refused to do a reasonable request?" I told him I didn't make the mess and no one else were asked to help sort it, just me. Scott lost it then "Alright you're suspended. Get you coat and clock out." All this in front of my mates…it was degrading and I felt humiliated.'

Nadeem stopped; it was clear he was emotional.

I paused for a second. 'Nadeem, thank you so much for that. It has really helped me understand the full events of the incident.' Nadeem dropped his head to his chest. 'So, Nadeem when does your next shift start?' I asked.

'Monday! Was supposed to be anyway. Honest, I would have helped clean up the mess; he just made me feel so uncomfortable,' Nadeem said.

'OK. Look Nadeem I will sort this out. We will see you back here Monday then,' I said. *

Nadeem looked up in surprise and Chris interjected,

'Well, who's going to speak with Rob and Scott? Make sure this poor boy doesn't get picked on again?'

'I will.' I declared.

Chris, being the good union representative he is, asked,

'So why can't Nadeem come in this weekend on overtime to make up the money he's lost?' Nadeem looked up again. 'Only if you want to Nadeem.' said Chris.

'Yes please' Nadeem replied.

'Good that's settled I will arrange it with Scott.' I smiled reassuringly and we all stood up.

'Welcome back Nadeem and again apologies for the distress this has caused you.'

We shook hands and Chris nodded his approval as they both left the room, or so I thought. Paula had her notepad laid out and was taking notes from the meeting. I paused to take stock and saw Chris was still hovering behind by my door. It was clear this wasn't done with and he closed the door behind him. His face was reddened and he was emotional.

'Now you see what we have to put up with! That poor boy was nearly in tears by the way he has been treated.'

'I know.' I confirmed. 'I will deal with it.'

'No Frank, we will deal with it. I want a face-to-face meeting with both Scott and Rob with Nadeem and you present, and they need to apologise'

'Well Chris, I need to speak with them first.'

'Nothing less than an apology will do,' Chris demanded. I felt myself bristling at his attitude because while I admired his dedication to the team, I value respect and politeness. I stood up and faced him squarely in the eye.

'Chris, I understand you're emotional and I respect you for supporting your members the way you do, but do not come into the GM office and lay down demands! I will work with you to secure this business but I am not going to take orders from you.' Chris pulled back; the message had been delivered so I softened my voice as I continued. 'Let me deal with its Chris. I need to think about how we arc going to resolve this issue with everyone intact; after all Nadeem and Rob have got to work together after this.'

Chris nodded.

'Well, I'm just worried; you haven't got much time, have you? Tomorrow, Friday and Nadeem back into work Saturday.'

'I know Chris, I know.'

Chris left the room and I turned to Paula who was looking a little concerned, it was the first time she had seen that side of me.

'Well, we need to get Scott up here.'

'I'll fetch him.' Paula left the room.

I sat and pondered; this could get out of hand if not tackled properly. Before long both Scott and Paula came into the office. Scott sat down and again I came away from my desk and sat with him and Paula.

'Thanks for coming Scott.' He sat in silence. 'We spoke to Nadeem today and I have a better understanding of what occurred on the day of the incident.'

'You mean his understanding?' Scott said forcefully.

'Yes, his understanding.' I placated. 'I have asked Nadeem to return to work as he is now off suspension.'

Scott glared.

'What do you mean? He refused a direct order from my team leader, his direct boss!'

'I know but we didn't really follow up correctly to log it all.'

Scott interrupted, 'No, I'm sorry I have got to support my team leader here. We cannot have people making up their own minds if they will do something or not. You have got to back me on this Frank! I told Rob I'm backing him. I've already assured Rob that Nadeem is not going back into the warehouse. Rob doesn't want him there.'

'Scott, I hear you but the manner in which this so-called reasonable request was given was not conducive to the normal protocol one would expect.'

Scott erupted, 'Bullshit! He didn't obey an order; that's the truth of it.' I sat in silence so Scott could calm down. Paula sat observing. I broke the silence.

'Obey? Order? Are these really the words you are using and trying to hide behind? Reasonable request and being asked?' Scott sat in silence. 'Scott, have you ever heard of unconscious bias?' Scott shook his head, so I continued,

'Unconscious bias is usually a behaviour towards a social stereotype about certain groups of people, which people are unaware they are exhibiting.' Scott looked confused so I continued. "Everyone holds unconscious beliefs about various social and identity groups and these biases usually come from the tendency to organise social worlds by categorising.' Scott still looked confused. "Ok tell me what the security guard looks like on nights?' I asked. Scott came out of his thoughtfulness.

'I don't know him.'

'Him? How do you know it's a him?' Scott looked perplexed. 'OK Scott what do you think the night security guard would look like if it was a him?' I asked. Scott thought for a second

'Well, I suppose late middle aged, retired even. Overweight, balding, white hair I guess.'

'Precisely. Without knowing it you described an unconscious bias to all security guards.'

I turned to Paula.

'Paula who have we got on nights for security.'

'Her name is Jenny and she's a graduate student studying physical biology. She is also a very competent kick boxer. She does security to earn a little more cash for her studies.'

I turned to Scott who was in silence.

'You see Scott if I asked you who was on reception you would unconsciously picture Jenny.'

Scott looked uncomfortable; clearly that exercise had hit a nerve and he was being proved wrong, for all the right reasons. 'Don't feel bad Scott, unconscious bias is far more prevalent than conscious prejudice and often incompatible to one's own conscious values. Certain scenarios can activate unconscious attitudes and beliefs. For example, bias is more prevalent when working under pressure.' I started to break down the facts.

'Rob was under pressure it was month end and he needed to get the lorries away. Correct?'

Scott nodded.

'I get why he didn't want Charlie to pick up his mess as he was the only fork lift truck driver there on the day. Correct?'

Scott nodded.

'Rob made the right decision, there's no doubt. However, he turned to the dispatch packers, there are four in all, and clicked his fingers at the only Indian guy there.'

Scott eyes widened. 'Hang on a minute Frank. Rob is not racist.'

'I know Scott,' I countered, 'however, he unconsciously turned to the only person that didn't fall into his own stereotypical group.' Scott sat back motionless. 'That happens as an unconscious decision when under extreme pressure. It's natural, I have no issues with the way Rob decided; I have an issue on how he asked.'

Scott looked puzzled. 'Scott, had you taken the appropriate steps in the investigation and asked the witnesses what happened and taken everyone statements you would have picked out the real issues. Rob humiliated and degraded Nadeem in front of his peers, colleagues and friends. That's the real issue here.'

'I've told Rob I am supporting him. I can't change that, Frank,' Scott declared.

'I know you did Scott, and that's before you knew all the facts. A valuable lesson here! So, our predicament now is Rob'

Scott's demeanour changed and he nodded in acknowledgement.

'Scott do me a favour. Go and ask Rob to come up here would you please?'

Scott stood up and left the room but with less swagger than when he came in.

Paula spoke, 'So, we have a team leader who thinks he has the full support of his manager. We've got the shop steward supporting the employee who's aggrieved. So how are we going to please everyone on this?'

Paula was soon becoming a trusted resource.

'I know, it's a tough one.' I said thoughtfully and honestly.

Within ten minutes Rob and Scott entered my office. They both sat at the table between Paula and myself.

'Paula could you fetch Chris please.'

I nodded to Paula and she left the room. Both Scott and Rob looked at each other. I sat with both of them biding time until the others appeared. I had one piece of paper in front of me.

'Thanks for coming Rob. I'm trying to find a way through on the incident that happened with Nadeem several weeks ago.'

'Yes, Scott said.' Rob's demeanour was cold and distant; a man of few words now, it would seem.

Chris and Paula walked into the room and both sat at the table so I wasted no time in getting to the point of the matter.

'Well Rob, I have heard from all concerned and would like to create an environment that both Nadeem and yourself can work together.'

As I was talking Rob's head was shaking negatively.

'Nadeem made me look like a proper idiot and undermined my authority, I cannot have him back on my shift.'

'Do you not think if you had taken a different way this could have been avoided? I mean clicking fingers and making someone pick up someone else's mess needs to be handled with a bit of tact? Especially in front of your peers, colleagues?'

Rob folded his arms and said nothing but just shook his head in denial.

Silence filled the room and it was clear Rob couldn't see what he could have done better. I picked up the A4 piece of paper and screwed it up.

'OK, well we can't seem to move from this impasse!'

Chris looked shocked; Paula confused. I then threw the screwed-up piece of paper across the room deliberately missing the waste paper bin. I turned to Rob clicked my fingers and said aggressively,

'Pick that up!' Rob looked at the piece of paper so I continued, 'Do it now Rob, come on,' clicking my fingers again. He actually began to rise from his seat to follow out the instruction but then paused and looked at Scott, his direct manager, the HR manager and the shop steward. 'Wait! You can't talk to me like…' he stopped talking and sat down.

'Yes, I can Rob, because I am your manager, I can make you do anything.' Rob took a breath and I immediately got up and walked across the room picked up the piece of paper and dropped it into the bin.

'Not nice is it Rob?' Rob lowered his head.

'I'm sorry I did that and made you look subordinate but I wanted you to have an idea of how it feels.' Rob looked up at me. 'Rob, you can't talk to people like that, and click your fingers and expect your team members to obey your command; you have to treat people with respect.'

'Yes, I understand now.'

We all adjourned and Nadeem returned for his overtime in the warehouse.

CHAPTER 6

A Lesson in Manners

One of the biggest challenges on this assignment was Scott Mullen. A driven man who always had what was best for the business at the forefront of his mind, or so, he thought and believed.

His outwardly aggressive stance and lack of communication with colleagues was a huge obstacle and I needed to overcome it. My head and gut told me he was worth saving, despite the opinions of others.

I was still working on the assumption that he, like so many other people, was not deliberately sabotaging the business through his actions and inactions. I began to wonder whether he was only responding to the situation. After all, production was the problem and it needed to be fixed. In my experience when people exhibit this type of behaviour it is for self-protection; a basic human response to the attacks happening on a daily basis. So, as part of my one-to-one process I rang him and asked to join his production meeting which he reluctantly accepted.

'Be there for 9am sharp in the production meeting,' he snapped before putting the phone down, which stirred little emotion in me. Indeed, I just needed to get to the bottom of his attitude and behaviour. I was actually looking forward to seeing how Scott managed the morning production meetings, but that was for tomorrow - I had other things to deal with and fix today.

I glanced at the clock; there was that two o'clock phone call with the customer I wanted to attend so I gathered my papers and mobile ready to observe, and made my way to the boardroom.

The boardroom had a large conference phone in the centre of the table. Daniel was seated and reaching over to dial the conference number. Alongside him was Salma, the Customer Services lead, and Heather, the Customer Services Account Manager. A young man was at the end of the table who I later found out was Charlie, the Planner for the area where this product was to be produced. All of them were nervous and apprehensive about the phone call. You could feel it in the air; a sense of intimidation and dread; not what you come to work for, that's for sure. The call dialled out and a voice barked from the speaker. It belonged to Nick Bate,s our difficult customer and head buyer. '

Who's there?'

'It's Daniel with Salma, Heather, Charlie and our new General Manager, Frank Walsh.'

'What another one?' The voice exclaimed! Daniel smiled.

'Yes, shall we continue?'

'Yes, alright then.'

'Salma can you give us an update please' asked Daniel.

'Yes, sure.' Salma was of Mediterranean background and looked very focused and efficient. She started to go through the lists of products. She'd only just started to reel off the part numbers that were to be dispatched in the week, before the voice on the other end interrupted.

'Am I going to get the 720 I asked for?' Silence in the room: Salma looked at Daniel for guidance.

'Well?' Barked the caller.

'Sorry no, we had problems with….' Salma started to explain, however the caller let out a sound of disgust.

'You have got to be joking?' he exclaimed. Once again silence in the room.

'What the fuck is going on over there. Don't you people have a clue what you're doing?'

Daniel leapt to Salma's defence.

'Nick! We're trying our best; we just had some production issues.'

I noticed no production colleagues were present.

'That's always the fucking excuse. I'm sick of it!' Daniel was about to respond when I gestured to him that I would take over. I leaned into the phone.

'Hi! It's Frank Walsh, the General Manager here.' Silence from the phone. 'Can I respectfully ask that you do not use that type of language to my staff, it's disrespectful.' A statement, certainly not a question and I paused, waiting for his response, which was swift.

'Are you for real?' he bellowed.

'Yes.' Again I stopped with that. Silence is a great tool if you use it correctly.

'This is bloody ridiculous' he continued. 'Do you have any idea what you are doing over there?'

'We are trying to explain to you what we are doing if you would allow Salma and the team to speak.'

'Go on then,' he barked.

Nervously Salma moved to the phone.

'The 720 you refer to will be late because the machine that produces it broke down. We can get some to you....' Again, an interruption.

'It's always breaking down it's a piece of shit. Why don't you get a new one or make the fucking thing work!'

I leaned into the phone.

'Nick, I have respectfully asked you not to speak to the team like that.' I paused.

'Well, what the fuck you going to do about it?'

'Nick can I ask you who your direct line manager is?' There was a long pause.

'Why do you want to know that?' he enquired.

'Because I need to inform them how you are representing your company to a strategic supplier.' There was a long pause again.

The room was in absolute silence. Each person was looking at each other, incredulous that this buyer had been silenced.

'Sorry Frank. I'm just under a lot of pressure due to your shortfall.'

'I quite understand. However, we are being honest and we are here to advise you on what we are doing to overcome the problem.'

A customer always remembers how you overcame a problem long after the problem has been forgotten.'

'OK, what do you have for me then?' he mellowed, almost asking respectfully.

Salma began to highlight the components they would be receiving and even Charlie contributed, stating when the 720 components would actually be scheduled in to be made. I left the room at that point nodding to Daniel, who just smiled and nodded a thank you back as I turned to close the door.

When people exhibit behaviours like bullying, most of the time it's because they themselves are under tremendous pressures and this is their coping mechanism. I'm sure outside of work, of this internal pressure they are all quite decent. It's rare you find someone who would genuinely enjoy exerting their strengths on innocent personnel. However, be aware, they do exist!

Remember too, there are two businesses working together. Individuals within that business are only representatives of the company. These people can come and go, but the businesses will still exist long after they have gone. Well, hopefully they do, if the business is successful.

As a leader or any form of people manager, you have to support your team at every level no matter what. Daniel learnt a valuable lesson as did Nick, the customer. I'd like to think his team had a better day due to my conversation and Nick thought about what I had said to him.

CHAPTER 7

Taking the Tiger by the Tail

The next day I woke refreshed, a spring in my step as I entered the office, anticipating the challenges which lay ahead. Scott's production meeting was number one on my list.

I arrived in good time as I certainly wasn't going to be late for this production meeting at any cost. I dutifully sat at the end of the large white table in the production office waiting for the participants. Five minutes to go, Scott walked in with coffee in hand and nodded an acknowledgement to me. He sat down and opened an A4 lined pad.

We waited!

Next to arrive at two minutes to nine was a plump middle-aged lady holding a bag of components in her hand, followed shortly by two older gentlemen covered in machine oil and grease - had to be maintenance as they always go around in pairs!

Gone nine and we were still sitting there, waiting. Two minutes passed and two girls strolled in with coffee in their hands followed by another guy. The meeting started at 9.07am precisely. I was there to observe and make notes but let me tell you, this wouldn't be happening at any meeting I would be leading. Scott opened the meeting.

'Right, what the hell happened on the night shift?' I inwardly winced.

One of the girls looked at her notes and stated that the key machine went down and there was no engineering support.

'Well, we were not called out!' fifty per cent of the maintenance team exclaimed defensively.

Scott scribbled down furiously.

'Mary what do you have?'

Mary passed the bag over and started to explain that they were defective parts from the previous shift.

Again, more defective parts.

Again, Scott started writing it all down. Time was passing and nothing was being done about the repeating issues, only reporting.

The door opened and a gentleman walked boldly in and sat down. No apology for running late or mindful of all the other people. He was holding what looked like a defective part in his hand. This was Graham Fearn, the engineering manager.

'A load of scrap from night shift again,' said Graham and slid the part across the table. Scott picked it up shaking his head in disbelief and sighing heavily.

'A blind man in a sand storm could see that!' he declared.

He started furiously scribbling down the issues as Graham took great delight, or so it seemed, in telling the story of the rejected parts from the night shift.

By the time Mary, Graham and the two engineers had finished complaining about everyone and everything it was nearly 10am. Scott, in all this time, was writing and huffing and puffing, taking hold of all the issues that everyone was throwing at him.

Another 45 minutes and the meeting closed. Scott was spent, exhausted and it was only just gone ten in the morning.

It was clear that Scott was taking everything on board and not letting anything go. I attended the production meetings for the next three days and the similar pattern occurred. What was even worse was that after Scott scribbled everything down the previous day he would start a new page the following day, without even reflecting back on what had gone before!

Then after the meeting, Scott stormed off for his usual cigarette break. I was left in the production room alone. This has got to stop, I thought.

Initially, I was going to observe for a week but I couldn't hold back any longer. I called Scott into my office on the Friday morning after watching this poor guy torture himself for four days.

Sheepishly Scott entered the room. I immediately stood up and walked around my desk to greet him at the meeting table. Paula was in attendance again making file notes.

'Hi Scott, thanks for coming. Sit down.' Scott sat quietly. 'Scott, I have been observing you and your team's interaction at the production meeting.' I paused for a moment to let him have a chance to breathe. 'I'd like to share some observations with you if I may.'

Scott just nodded. This was totally uncharacteristic of Scott and I sensed he felt he was in trouble, if not going to be let go. Once I sensed this I jumped up. 'Fancy a coffee?'

He looked up slightly surprised and nodded with a shrug.

'How do you take it?'

'White, no sugar.' he declared.

'Same as me, sweet enough, right?' I tried to smile but he just stared at me.

You have to diffuse any situation like this if you sense the person is uncomfortable. After all, offering a coffee to someone you're about to fire is unheard of, right? Unless you're one of those power-hungry maniacs, which I wasn't, but Scott still wasn't sure what I was, or what my agenda might be.

Never abuse your position or station, no matter what the circumstances. There's always a way through these difficulties.

'So, Scott I'd like to offer an alternative way of running your daily production meetings if I may.'

I felt there was no point highlighting his errors, better to offer him a positive solution.

'What do you have in mind?' he asked inquisitively.

'A Daily Management System or DMS whereby all the participants arrive on time, with all the correct KPI's and feed you information that you can make informed decisions on.'

'How does that work Frank?' he asked.

Greeted with less resistance than I thought I began;

'Every day at 10am people attend in a stand-up area on the shop floor. Each attendee must have their own KPI and report on it. They have enough time from when they arrive in the morning to 10am to get this information ready.'

Scott raised his eyebrows but nodded, agreeing.

'Your production meeting currently lasts for an hour with nine people in attendance so the DMS should take no longer then ten minutes.'

'Ten minutes!' exclaimed Scott 'Never!'

'Well, it can be, let's say 30 minutes. What if I said we could get your meeting down to 30 minutes?' Scott still scoffed at this but I carried on.

I then drew the board layout on the white board and for an hour we engaged in healthy debate about who should be in attendance and what KPI's they should bring to the area. We agreed the area and mocked up a large magnetic white board using tape and marker pens.

Month							Owner				On Time
Week No							Deputy				Late
Target (Sales)											New
Attendance	M	T	W	T	F	ACTION	Owner	Deadline	Status	URGENT - DO IT NOW	
Health & Safety											
Finance											
Quality											
Customer Services											
Operations											
Engineering											
Human Resources											
Last 24 Hours	Target	Actual	Delta			ACTION PLAN				Actions greater than 2-weeks	
LTIs MTD											
Sales Invoiced MTD											
Stock Turns											
Owed debt											
Open Complaints											
OTIF-R											
OTIF-P											
Mass Balance Waste											
Net Waste											
OEE (Extrusion)											
OEE (Print)											
OEE (Finishing)											
OEE (Building Film)											
Unauthorised Absence											

THIS IS YOUR PRIORITY TODAY

Above is a finished article.

Any visual management board is only useful if it changes a behaviour. Having a whole area with reams of charts is meaningless and is effectively just wall paper. I worked in a business whereby weeks of work and inputting data had to be put into highly visible graphs. No one even looked at it and it became a farce - even the customers weren't bothered. To measure it is to manage it, fair enough, but to over-complicate it becomes ineffective. You cannot drive forward looking in the rear-view mirror. This DMS method gives ownership and responsibility.

'Scott, the discipline of the DMS is crucial. Using a RAG system (Red for late. Amber for New and Green for on time) highlights very quickly what is happening to the business. It only records the last twenty-four hours and looks forward to the next twenty-four hours. Don't get bogged down in detail. By 10am everyone should know their numbers. This is an escalation reporting structure, that's all. By all means capture actions that need to be taken off-line. The bottom right-hand corner gives us that capability with everything of more than two weeks duration.'

Scott nodded in approval.

'Starting on Monday, open with the register. 10am by your watch, have a roll call. If no one is in attendance on time or even if they turn up late, they receive a red magnet.'

Scott smiled, but I could see it was one of disbelief.

'It works trust me.'

'I would love to see Graham, the Engineering Manager, turn up for anything on time!'

'Oh, he will,' I spoke.

'So, what happens the next day if they're late?' Scott asked.

'Right well they get another red mark, then in front of all your colleagues you ask them to stay behind.' Scott nodded. 'When everyone has gone, then you ask if there's something wrong. Can I help? What's the problem?'

'I see; so more supportive than chastising?'

'Precisely. However the rest of the team don't know that; they are thinking they are having a right bollicking.'

'What happens if they get three reds in a row?'

'Then it's a competency issue and should be processed through the HR channels. In all the time I have been using this methodology it's never got to that stage, trust me.'

I moved back to the DMS Board.

'When the roll call has been entered go over to the right-hand side of the white board: Urgent, do it now.'

'It's all urgent,' Scott mused.

'This is for only if there a real emergency that will stop the customer receiving their product tomorrow. Such as a supplier not delivering or machine break down that needs to be resolved that day!'

Then I turned to the KPI's.

'Always first is the health and safety of everyone on site so we measure Lost Time Accidents. These are due to an accident at work which has prevented the person from returning to work. We have a zero target and we measure it every day.' Scott nodded.

'The next KPI is Sales invoiced month to date. Now, we have a budget target for the working month, don't we?'

'Yes, it's three point eight million.'

'Correct. So how many working days do we have in the month?'

'Twenty-two this month but it can vary from twenty to twenty-three,' Scott explained.

I drew up the figures on the whiteboard; '£3.8m divided by 22, the average working days in the month gives us a daily target of £172k a day.'

Scott did some quick calculations. 'Agreed.'

'This means that on day four of the month we should have invoiced £690k.'

'Yes' Scott agreed.

'So, if we track it by a daily graph with a linear target line we can see very quickly how far ahead or behind we are; therefore we don't wait until the end of the month to find out that we missed the target. This affords us the opportunity to fix the problem early on in the month when we have the time to do so.'

Scott smiled, the penny was dropping.

'What's a stock turn?' Scott enquired as this was the next KPI on the board.

'A stock turn is how many times in a month or year you turn the stock over and replenish it. It's the total amount of stock divided by the total amount of sales going out the door.'

'What does this give us?'

'Well, every business needs cash. Cash is the life blood of any business. Without it, it will collapse so you have to measure where all that cash is going.'

'I see,' Scott said, but I could see he didn't really fully understand. I noted to myself that a course of Finance for Non-Finance managers was needed. I decided to use a different approach.

'It's the same as measuring owed debt. This is the cash we as a company have not yet received from the customers, despite the fact that we have paid for all the materials and labour to make the product. So prudently, we measure the debt owed to us so we can recovery it through accounts receivables.'

Scott understood this one more.

'So, the customers haven't paid up then?'

'Precisely! Do you know how much this company is owed?'

'No, why would I?'

'Well, it's over three million pounds!'

'Wow!' Scott exclaimed. 'That's a lot of money.'

'Yes, and we are owed it. It's ten percent of our turnover. With no cash coming into the business, we cannot pay wages or pay for stock.'

'Your fees!' Scott laughed and I had to smile with him, he was loosening up. Dare I say he was enjoying the education? Only time would tell; we carried on reviewing the new KPI's.

'Open complaints. These are complaints our customers have made against us that we haven't responded to, or found the root cause of the issues.'

'I see. How many do we have open?'

'You mean you don't know?' I smiled, raising an eyebrow as again I saw Scott starting to see the picture. 'That's why it's now on the board. We currently have twenty-three open complaints; some going back months.'

'Months? I didn't know.'

'Well from now on we're going to measure it daily. We're going to introduce the 5+5+5 rules. Five days to acknowledge to the customer we have logged the complaint. Five days to investigate the complaint. Five days to resolve the issue found from the investigation and get back to the customer with the result. That way we will only ever have open no more than fifteen days of complaints at any given time.'

'That's impressive,' Scott acknowledged. 'OTIF R and P?' he asked.

"Yes, so OTIF is On Time In Full Delivery and a barometer whereby *we can gauge whether or not* we are servicing the customer correctly. The reason I'm introducing OTIF R. The R is the request date from the customer to us. OTIF P is the planned date we acknowledge back to the customer. We measure both, because we have to be mindful of the market conditions. If our lead times are so far out and we are not servicing the customer they will eventually go elsewhere. They won't tell us they are leaving either, they will just go. We need to put processes in place to ensure we meet the customers requested dates and not our own planned date.'

'So, if the variances are so far out, we will have missed the boat?'

'Correct. So many companies stick rigidly to their own lead times because their processes have not been kept up to date with the ever-changing market out there.'

'When can we roll this out then?' asked Scott.

'When do you want to?' I asked.

'Well, we've got to get the board printed out and the layout and everything. Could take weeks.'

I smiled - still a lot to learn here.

'No Scott. Let's just do this mock up with black tape and roll it out on Monday. JFDI I call it. Give people enough time to know what's coming. Let me chair the DMS for the first week or so, then, when we are happy with the format we can go into print. We will make adjustments.'

'Take me through it again. I can roll this out and if you don't mind, I'll give it a try myself.'

I was delighted with Scott. He was taking ownership of this new process and driving it forward. I gave him the overview again.

'The DMS board is the final tier in what is a three to four tier process. This is the board that all the heads of departments attend. You will notice that on the header there is an owner of the board and a deputy. Each head of department must nominate a deputy. The deputies only stand in when the responsible head of department is off site. There is no excuse for the deputy to be there otherwise.

At the bottom of the board in bold red letters is THIS IS YOUR PRIORITY TODAY! It means exactly that. Do not go to meetings, do not go back to your desk to replicate emails, get on and fix the problem. Once the roll call is carried out then remember to go straight over to the URGENT DO IT NOW board. This is dedicated to anything that's going to stop the business in the next 24 hours.

Then go to the KPI. You will notice that they are in the same sequence order as the register of attendance.

Anything which is of a negative variance must be reported and an action plan raised. Now it's very important that you do not make more than one person responsible for that action to be reported back to the team the following day.'

'But it may take more than that person to sort it' Scott exclaimed.

'Yes, but this is the ownership for the reporting back of the details of what has occurred.'

'I see.'

I went on to explain,

'Never put more than one person to any actions that comes from the DMS. The reason for this is a little story about four people named Everybody, Somebody, Anybody, and Nobody.'

Scott smiled. He was starting to like my anecdotes because he could relate to them. It's easy to make things difficult, but difficult to make things easy.

'There was an important job to be done and Everybody was sure that Somebody would do it.

Anybody could have done it but Nobody did it.

Somebody got angry about that, because it was Everybody's job.

Everybody thought that Anybody could do it but Nobody realized that Everybody wouldn't do it.

It ended up that Everybody blamed Somebody when Nobody did what Anybody could have done.'

Scott laughed, 'Got it!'

I believed he was getting it; he was a different person to the one I first met.

We spent more than an hour going step by step through the sequence of the board, and Scott was ready to launch it.

Monday morning. It was just before 10am and Scott was quiet but his fingers were drumming the underside of the table. Under the calm was a nervous man keen to get this working. I stood next to Scott and everyone turned up on time for DMS; even Graham Fearn, the engineering manager was in attendance.

Scott opened the meeting brilliantly, going through the sequence as discussed. He was quick to stop any deep discussion on a particular topic, explaining that this wasn't a talking shop, it was a reporting and action shop. Then the team had their first official stand up.

'Health and safety?'

'Here,' said Jason

'Quality?' Continued Scott

'Here,' I turned to see Sarah

'Customer service?'

'Here,' said Salma.

'Operations?'

'Here,'

'Engineering?'

'Here,'

'Finance?' There was silence. Scott turned around, acknowledged no presence and placed a red magnetic disc on the finance column.

'HR?'

'Here,'

Scott continued on the board.

'Right is there anything at this time that's going to stop us delivering to our customers?'

Silence; Scott continued the daily routine.

'Any lost time accidents in the last twenty-four hours?'

'None!' Jason cried.

'Excellent. Any customer complaints in the last twenty-four hours?'

'No,' declared Salma.

'Invoice month to date against the target?'

'Three seven five against the target of three one two so we are sixty-three up! Good.'

'Any machine breakdowns?'

'All good,' declared Graham proudly

'No finance, so we don't know the stock situation.' I noted their absence and would speak with Stuart, the Finance Director, after finishing all the daily management stand ups which culminated the morning.

'Any unplanned absences?' Asked Scott.

'One, night shift, and we will be calling them at two o'clock today to ensure that they are back in tonight.'

Scott closed the meeting. He completed the board, turned around and thanked everyone for their time and input. It took less than twenty minutes to understand what had happened in the last twenty-four hours and what was going to happen in the next twenty-four hours.

He tasked all the right people with their actions to be achieved within that working day. All Scott did was write on the board the dates the people committed to (never tell people the date and time they should have something completed by) as there's no true ownership.

When it was completed and the group had disbanded, everyone hurrying away to do what they were now tasked with, Scott walked over to me.

'You were wrong, Mr. Walsh.'

'Wrong!?' I said surprised.

'Yes, that meeting took eighteen minutes, not thirty!' He smiled, looked very relaxed, and said, 'C'mon I need to buy you a coffee as I've got time now!'

'Good, so now we have more time because you have delegated the workload. I believe I said ten minutes.' I smiled at him and he laughed. 'Are you able to support Daniel and his team with the customer conference calls?' Scott smile disappeared.

'With that bully Nick Carter?'

'I think you'll find he's become a bit more amenable.'

'I'll take your word for it, but sure, OK.'

Part of the DMS development is then to tier down to the previous level on the shop floor. I tasked Scott with that and he really did a good job. He made it his own by introducing RAG magnets with facial expressions on. Emoji's. Really did make us all smile.

I often find that by establishing good working practices in one area it soon becomes contagious. Other departments establish the same ways of working. When I am hunting out the foxes in the organization, I give the main suspects the benefit of the doubt. By taking time and mentoring I managed to save Scott and his reputation. He wasn't a fox he was a very frustrated rabbit; now his frustration had turned to something positive.

Only a week into the new DMS and finance still hadn't attended. By the following week I found myself stomping towards finance. I was a little cross, true visual management drives a behaviour everywhere. Except in finance, it seemed!

I arrived in the finance department where Stuart and his team were on yet another conference call to the central finance function. As I entered, Stuart looked up and immediately saw my expression. He checked his watch, it was way past the allotted time; he silently gestured to the live conference call that was on-going.

He shrugged his shoulders and I gestured to him to call me when he was finished. I left the room slamming the door.

Within the hour a sheepish Stuart entered my office. He closed the door behind him (my door being always open to encourage people to feel that they can enter) .

'Sorry Frank but you know what it's like,' he gestured towards the phone.

'No Stuart, tell me what it is like?' I decided it was time to sort this out. I was not going to put up with excuses.

'Well, you know,' spluttered Stuart. 'They all insist on these calls.'

'Stuart, I do not care for the faceless finance fraternity obsession. They need constant reassurance with the numbers despite the fact that I give a forecast every week. You are supposed to be part of the plant team. Everyone sees it, except you. You either want to be part of the plant team or you want to be part of the central function. You need to make up your mind what it is you want.'

'Of course, I want to be part of the team, you know that, but they are so demanding.'

'Matrix management is about managing it.'

'But how do I do that? I'm between a rock and a hard place.' The inference was there; I relaxed. Part of management is managing the expectations of your manager. It's always a skill.

'Can I make a suggestion?' I asked.

'Sure, please.'

'Use Outlook Calendar to block out the DMS slot. Block it for no end date, then give access to Dave, your matrix boss, so he can view your calendar for appointments. He will acknowledge that and when he tries to book a timeslot with you, he'll see when you're busy and will automatically choose a timeslot when you're free.'

Stuart agreed, so I continued, 'This way, they still think they are in charge without realizing you have directed them.'

Stuart looked visibly relieved that he was getting help and nodded graciously. 'It won't happen again Frank, I can assure you.'

'Let's see how it works. It will be good; then the team will know you're a team player and not a central lap dog.'

Stuart left the room, rushing I suspected to his Outlook calendar.

CHAPTER 8

Time is Money

I sat back in my chair looking out of the window on a sunny afternoon. People hurrying around outside. One figure I noticed in particular - Mark Winters, the Sales Director - rushing towards my office.

Mark had a face like thunder when he entered my office. I looked up shuffling some papers on my desk, staying calm, as usual.

'What's the matter?'

'Another customer let down after I promised them it wouldn't happen again!'

'Give me the details and I will investigate.'

Mark gave me the works order number and all the details. I walked into the planning office to see Daniel at his desk reading his emails. I leaned over his shoulder.

'178 unread emails!' I spluttered out.

'Yes, I know,' sighed Daniel uncharacteristically.

'Well, can you give me some background on this order please?' Daniel took the piece of paper and without reading all of it he spoke. 'Yes, this is the Julian order. We told Mark we couldn't do this when he wanted it but he went back to the customer and committed to it.'

'I see.' I didn't see, I clearly wasn't being told all the facts. In my experience there are always many sides to a story.

'OK, can you and the team come up with the next planned date for delivery? I'll talk to Mark.'

'Will do.'

'Oh, and by the way when you have done that pop along to my office and bring your laptop.'

'Laptop?' enquired Daniel.

'Yes, Daniel. You're going to get a crash course in the rules of email.' Daniel smiled in relief. I returned to my office. An hour later Daniel popped his head around my door, laptop in hand.

'Hi, is it convenient?'

'Sure,' I said and once again left my desk and greeted Daniel at the table. He sat down and displayed his laptop.

'OK,' I said, 'give it here.'

He dutifully passed it over. I then went into his emails which had grown to 203 unread emails since the last time we spoke.

'203 unread emails!'

'I know,' said Daniel, rather embarrassed.

I clicked on select all and then right clicked and deleted all in front of Daniel. His face was incredulous! You would have thought I had just ripped of his right arm. Wide mouthed he looked at me as I was smiling. He was speechless.

'Right, the first lesson in email management.'

I stood up and on the clean white board I wrote 208.

Daniel was still reeling from my action and he just kept staring at an empty inbox. He looked at me then back at the screen. I closed the top of the laptop so he was no longer distracted. He turned to me, still wide eyed.

'How long does it take you to read an email?' I asked

'Depends on the length I guess' said Daniel, now coming back into the real world. 'Couple of minutes?'

'Let's say a minute; so that's 208 minutes.' I referred to the board. 'Let's say it takes another minute to reply.' I wrote on the board "208 +208 = 416 minutes". So as of today, you have 416 minutes of email traffic. Correct?'

Daniel looked at his closed laptop forlornly and uttered, 'Well not now I haven't!'

I laughed, 'so how many work hours is that?' I wrote on the board; 416 / 60 = 7 hours. 'That's a working day,' I declared. 'And that's if they respond to your emails and you reply back.'

Daniel acknowledged the working day number.

'Daniel. Emails are time bandits. They take up unnecessary time where you would be better off doing something else.' Daniel nodded. 'How many emails do I have in my inbox do you think?'

Daniel smiled. 'Well, you're the General Manager. You have the board to report to, customers and colleagues. I'd say…. around 100.'

I went to my desk and turned my screen around. There were three un-read emails in my inbox. Daniel's face reverted to an expression of incredulity.

'So how do we get the time back?' I went back to the board. 'There are five rules to email management. First when you come into work in the morning open up your emails and go and get a coffee, wait until the email has replicated and then return.' I wrote "Your Priorities" on the board and continued.

'Rule 1. Click on who and start with your boss first. They would be rare, but if one is hidden within 200 others you may not get to it during your working day. That could be problematic especially if your boss is asking for information, they need to be elevated up to declare at an important meeting.'

Daniel nodded in agreement and, it seemed, recognized that dilemma.

'Then click on alphabetically and look at all your direct reports. They may require your help, perhaps they're stuck on an issue for the next DMS meeting. Next, click onto major customers you are aware of in case there are emergencies you have to deal with. After that ignore the rest. These will be for information only, or reports which you can read or not.'

Daniel finally spoke, 'Yes. I see the logic in that and you're right. Most of the emails are fyi.'

'Well, you know what fyi stands for?'

'For your information?' Daniel said confidently thinking I was patronizing him.

'No, I said it's f#@* you instead!'

Daniel laughed out loud. A bit too loud, I think he was becoming manic.

I wrote on the board the number two.

'Rule Two. Never send an email to more than one direct contact.' I then recited the "Everybody, Somebody Nobody and Anybody" parable.

'The Third Rule. Never carbon copy CC and delete the BCC icon from your email. CC are only there for protection reasons, nothing more than that. It's so people can say, "well I did copy you" when things go wrong.'

'The Fourth Rule. Never answer an email with a question. This creates a ping pong effect which is compounded if you copy people into it. That's why you don't copy; if it's that important pick up the phone, or better still, go and talk to the person asking the question.' Daniel nodded.

'The Fifth Rule. At the end of every working day empty your inbox either by filing all the emails you want to keep or deleting them as I have just done.' I sat down with Daniel at the table and opened his laptop and there were three emails in his in box.

'Now using the five rules, what would you do with these new emails?' I asked.

Daniel scanned them and to my delight he deleted them all. 'All three were definitely fyi'. We both laughed.

'So, when you go on you holidays you put an out of office note right? Well, when you return create a folder with your holiday dates and move all emails into that folder.'

'But that's hundreds.' Daniel gasped.

'I know, but if they were important trust me, they will ring you as they know you're back. All you say is "sorry haven't got around to it, can I help now?"

'Another good thing to save time and emails is allow all your work colleagues access to your calendar and vice versa.'

'Why?' Daniel pondered.

'Well, a lot of time is wasted just emailing between work colleagues setting up meetings. If you have access to their calendars you can work out exactly when everyone will be free for the meeting and send a meeting request for that time. Saves a lot of time.' I paused. I could see Daniel taking it all in.

'At my last assignment I was copied into a string of emails from five senior managers trying to organize a meeting. It was a farce. Eventually after fourteen emails, and hours of ping pong, I picked the phone up and asked them to stop sending me these ridiculous emails.'

'I see; makes sense.' Daniel acknowledged.

'Time is the currency of your life. Only you can spend it; don't let anyone else spend it for you.'

Daniel subsequently followed all these rules religiously and found he had taken control of his time. He measured that he got back two hours per day. That's ten hours a week - 40 hours a month. That's a whole working week.

When he went on holiday for two weeks he returned to 536 emails! He placed them into a folder. Only two people got back to him during his first week back!

CHAPTER 9

Sales v Ops

There are many conflicts in the world. Coca Cola vs Pepsi, Rangers and Celtic, Liverpool and Manchester United, but not many can hold up against Sales and Operations.

An unstoppable force meets an immovable object, it seems. The Sales are of course, the unstoppable force, driving orders to compensate their salaries with commission. The immovable object is Operations who do not want to change too much at short notice because it's not productive to do so.

Compromise and balance are the order of the day. I entered the sales office where Mark was sitting with Rachel, going through some statistics for the next meeting of the sales team.

'Hi Mark, I got the date for that order you asked about.'

'Great, 'he said, clearly a lot calmer than he had been when he entered my office that morning.

'It will be delivered to them on Monday's shipment.'

'Thanks, I'll let Julian know.'

I sat down opposite Mark. 'Julian was told it was Monday but for some reason he told the customer this Friday?' Mark looked puzzled. 'What reason would he have to do that, do you think?'

Mark shook his head. 'No idea' I paused for effect. I just wanted to let Mark absorb the fact that one of his team ignored a member of the operation team and also gave false information to a valued customer.

'May I suggest something?'

'Yes, sure' Mark said.

'While we are in this situation can sales and operations work together to create a red-hot list?'

'Red hot list?'

'Yes, a list of orders that must go out during a rolling fixed five-day planning cycle. No changes, no false promises. Your team's responsibility is to not change the order; after all, they have chosen it and my team is to deliver on the new red-hot list.'

'But we want it all.'

'Well reality says you can't have it all, so we have to be the grown-ups here and agree between sales and ops. Mark, people are concerned about what's going to happen. We are the seniors on this site, there cannot be a fag paper's difference in the messages we each give.'

I stopped and waited for a reaction.

Mark thought for a second, 'OK, let's create the red-hot list. I will tell my guys but they won't like it'.

'I know, but when we deliver on the first fixed five days we will then deliver on the next, and the next, and so on. Confidence will start to grow again.'

'How does it work?' Mark quizzed.

I sat opposite Mark and began,

'When a company finds itself in this situation, where demand outgrows supply due to poor scheduling, bad implementation of ERP or a catastrophic machine failure, then sales and ops form a team. I know, unheard of, right? So that's why we will form the "red hot list". It's a list made up by the sales team. It is a fixed five-day list of all the orders that have to be a must have.'

'They are all must haves!' exclaimed Mark.

'Of course, but the reality is we cannot get all of them done. As a business we need to make informed choices on which customers are going to get the product this working week.'

Mark nodded.

I continued, 'Who better than you Mark to know which key accounts we need to service while we get out of this mess? We will work together on the list and we will review it on a rolling five-day cycle, adding to the list as and when the product is dispatched. Your role is to set the list. My goal is to expedite it. We will meet once a week, Monday is usually best, because then we can address what has been produced over the weekend.' Mark was now listening intently.

'So, I cannot change anything for five days?'

'You can change the plan to add in anything you want to on the sixth day. As I say, it's a rolling five days. We must be seen as one here, Mark. We cannot have the Sales team coming down on the floor and demanding a change. You have to be strong here.'

'Yes, I see, but it's not going to be easy. You know how the team is about protecting their customers.'

'I agree, but these are the company customers, Mark; we have to work together. You will have to be fair on what you decide.'

'How will I know how much capacity we have?'

'Good question. I devised the rough-cut capacity plan into a unit of measure. We know the unit of measure from the orders. So, we tote them up and issue the works orders to the shop floor. I've based the efficiency level at eighty per cent, if we can do better, we will produce more.'

'So, the red-hot list is issued on a Monday every week?'

'Yes, and we will measure on time delivery to that list. Once I open up the efficiency we can revert back to original lead-times.'

'I see. OK it's worth a go.'

'Mark,' I pause for effect, 'I cannot stress the importance of us being united. Remember, we must stay strong and we will pull through this. I am relying on you to keep your department focused, too. We will work as a team as and when we deliver to the plan.'

Mark stood up and stretched out his hand,

'You can rely on me, just don't let me down Frank.'

I smiled. No, I won't.' I was confident enough in this process and I knew it would work but we needed to have the discipline.

Now we had to open up the capacity of the plant.

I stood up and left the room. Time was ticking. I knew it was a matter of days before real results were required to be seen. I needed to get ready for the senior stakeholders of this business, the big boys, or as I call them "The grown-ups".

I deliberated for the rest of the morning about what the key performance indicators should be. I went to see Scott and called for Daniel to come to his office. He obliged without hesitation and I was standing up, ready to deliver a speech that would focus my two key resources on the measures.

'Measures are used as a weapon, Dr. W. Edwards Deming said, but we need to drive fear out of the work place. Many performance measurement systems do exactly the opposite. When management does act on a metric, they don't look at the business process. Instead, they focus on someone, some other department or some outside factor to "blame". This causes people to game the system and to point their fingers elsewhere when problems arise. People want to see KPIs or Key Performance Indicators, or as I call them, Kick People Incessantly!' They both laughed and nodded agreement, so I continued,

'You must be data driven to make informed decisions,' I declared. 'Think about the KPI you are running at the moment; OTIF (on time delivery in full). Have you really completed a full order of product paperwork installation on time? No, we move the dates as we know we cannot deliver on time but because it's a KPI we fudge it, move it and give it a new date.'

Daniel looked at Scott accusingly and commented, 'That's exactly what they were doing.'

Scott opened his mouth to defend Operations but I quickly began talking before he could start.

'Inputs equals outputs so, measure Adherence to Schedule ATS. If that is right then OTIF will automatically fall out.'

'Always measure trends not just results,' I continued. I was on my soap box now. 'With the wrong Key Performance Indicators, the wrong measurement breeds the wrong behaviours. Health and Safety is a good measure of morale, correct?' They both nodded listening intently. 'It's everyone's right to go home safe from work but I pushed my senior management into demanding zero Lost Time Accidents.'

'I was wrong!' They both looked surprised. It's good to show your colleagues that you are not infallible. 'I created the behaviour of brushing it under the carpet and not showing the real problems.'

'So, I changed the KPI and I asked the managers to give me as many near misses reports in a month. As we know, near misses prevent future accidents. You see, a change in KPIs can drive the right change in behaviours. You know what happened, guys? We got all the near miss and hazard reports; we drove the root causes and put in fixes. As a direct result of that input, the output was no LTA.'

'You cannot manage without measurements. Do them daily. That's where the daily management system comes into play,' I continued well and truly on my soap box now.

'Show me how I am measured and I will show you how I perform. Human nature would drive you to do everything that's necessary to avoid losing your targets and, in some cases even driving people to falsify statistics to support their wrong KPI.'

'Let me tell you a true story from one of my previous roles. Once I worked for a tyrannical boss whose nickname was Wobbly Wainwright. He would erupt without warning at the slightest provocation. My colleagues would urge me on as I had no fear of the man, but I could see he was promoted above his capacity. To be fair his eruptions were due to stress, but he was a formidable character; imagine a great white shark with PMT if you will.'

'Tony, a cell manager, had to produce a certain amount of product per day and part of the process was a 24hr soak chamber. In this chamber the product required electrical current in a temperature -controlled environment to pass its final test. He had a KPI of 22 daily targets.'

'This poor manager was being driven by the wrong KPI so he religiously counted all the units in the soak chamber in order to hit the daily target, even though it wasn't packed, or even tested or quality checked. This was risky because if any of the units failed the final test the number was already declared. Now I could see that this was a critical path regarding the number of units in the soak chamber. However, I also knew that with only a limited capacity of 20 in the chamber you could only optimize 20 per 24hrs, so the daily target of 22 was never going to be achieved. The driver was the KPI of 10% improvement enforced by Wobbly Wainwright!'

'So, for me, the phrase "it's all in the soak chamber" has become attributed to the unrealistic KPIs which eventually drive the wrong behaviour. Needless to say, it caught up with him and I shall never forget the production meeting where the reality struck home to everyone when the director stood up and bellowed….

'How many in the soak chamber?'

'148!' was the meek reply.

(C)John Paul Reeves, 2011

'It must have been the only soak chamber which was the size of a small country.' Scott and Daniel smiled, but I continued, 'Tony was disciplined; the customer was let down and as a result Tony's self-confidence began to waiver and he began to fail consistently afterwards.'

'The end of the story was that Wobbly Wainwright was "promoted" (moved) to the side and on my subsequent appointment I made it clear - no lies, speak with data and above all, measure trends, not results.'

'What happened then, boss?' asked Scott.

'So, I started to measure Work in Progress (WIP) and invoiced only what was packed. This gave me insight into what was coming in and out of the soak chamber and by when. Measuring the right KPI led to more confidence in the data. In the end, we could justify further investment for a second soak chamber. The correct KPI for this scenario was "Amount Invoiced" and "WIP", not daily output against an unrealistic target.

'And Tony, The cell manager? What happened to him?' enquired Daniel.

'He regained his confidence and went on to become a very good operation director in his own right. To me that's the best bit, supporting and mentoring individuals.' I caught the eye of Scott; he knew I was referring to him. I closed my speech. 'So, team, what's the KPI we are going to drive ourselves to when Sales give us their red-hot list?'

They looked at each other collectively and said: 'Adherence to their schedule.' I think that was the first time Sales and Operations had agreed on anything in a long time.

'Correct!' I smile; the atmosphere had lightened between these two. They had come a long way in their relationship and in their individual growth. I was proud of Mark, and Scott was seeing a new approach.

Close of business and I was busy deleting all my emails. Always practice what you preach.

A sheepish Sarah, the Quality Manager entered my office.

'Can I have a word?' she asked meekly.

'Of course, come in, please sit down.' She did so tentatively. I moved from behind my desk, closed the door and sat opposite her.

She looked concerned so I tried to lighten the tension by asking if she wanted coffee.

'No thanks, 'she paused; 'I've been a bit worried about the stability of the site for some time.'

I nodded, remembering two ears one mouth.

'Well, I don't know if you know this, but my husband also works here. He's on shifts.'

'No, I didn't know.'

'Well with both of us working for the same business if it was to fail, we would be devastated.' I nodded in agreement.

She paused; 'I've been offered an opportunity outside of the Plant.' Again, I nodded. 'Well, I don't really want to leave as it's so convenient with my location and the kid's school run and all.'

'So,' I asked 'What is it you want to do?'

She sat back and sighed, 'I don't really know.'

'I see,' I said. 'Well, every time an important decision comes into my life, whether it's professional or personal, I go by three things.' Sarah looked up intently. 'Your Head, Your Heart and your gut.' I held up three fingers to illustrate.

'First your head, that's logic pure and simple, black and white what does that tell you about the decision. Secondly is your heart, full of emotion, even excitement about the decision you're going to make, and then finally your gut, experience or instinct. What does that tell you?' Sarah listened intently.

'Now I have found that whatever permutation the three give me, if two of them are telling me to do something then that's what I always go with and it hasn't let me down ever.' Sarah nodded.

I started to prompt her. 'What does your head say?'

'Well, there are two of us working in the same business which is in recovery mode and we need to mitigate the risks if it closes down' I nodded in agreement

'That's logical,' I said. 'What about your heart?'

She thought, then spoke. 'I love it here! I love the people and the job. I get a lot of satisfaction out of it. However, not lately as it's been stressful for everyone.'

'I can understand that.' I raised the third finger 'Gut?' I asked. Again, she thought a little.

'I don't know why but my gut tells me to stay as we will turn it around.' I nodded.

'What's the answer, do you think?'

'Well, two out of three is telling me I should stay.' I smiled, Sarah looked relieved, and she clearly was torn by a major decision.

'All I can assure you, Sarah, is that we will turn this around and we will be secure. I cannot change the past, only the future.'

Sarah sat thoughtfully nodding. She stood up.

'Thank you, Frank, for taking the time, it really helped me to think long and hard about the decision.'

'You're welcome.' I stood up and Sarah left the room.

Sarah stayed on and became the most successful Quality Manager within the division. The business was all the better for it and she was given a salary increase as a result.*

A few days later I did the usual daily routine of going to every daily management system. Starting promptly at 9am, then walking around the factory to hear all the departments' DSM's until I had completed the final and fourth tier in my open planned offices. I sat back at my desk and poured a coffee as Helen, the PA, rushed in.

'Have you heard? They're coming over?' Slightly startled I looked up and asked.

'Who's coming over?'

'The owners! The Americans!'

'When?' I enquired.

'Next Monday. They sent an agenda to Andrew.'

'Great! Then when he's happy to share it, we will respond.' Helen was taken aback by my nonchalant attitude so I reassured her.

'Helen, the closest I get to panic is picnic.' She smiled and left the office. I casually put my safety shoes on and walked towards the Gemba.

Now as I walked, I was thinking. Of course, my heart leapt a little when I heard the news but I wasn't going to make a fuss. But…. what are we going to prepare for the grown-ups?

As it turned out I didn't have long to ponder as Andrew dropped a message into my inbox later that day announcing that I had another meeting to deal with prior to the Americans.

The European business consisted of seven plants. Each plant had a member of the Executive leadership team running it and they had all arranged to visit us pending the USA arrival. There was a flurry of excitement for the rest of the week. I was amused to observe the inflated sense of importance and ceremony engendered by the forthcoming visit.

Was I going to be asked to raise the bunting? Alert the media? Polish the gravel?

I too, eagerly anticipated their arrival but kept uncharacteristically quiet about my thoughts. The truth was that it could go either way and I knew what was potentially at stake here. We had made improvements, there was no doubt about that, but was it enough?

CHAPTER 10

Lockdown

The morning of their arrival I sat in the boardroom with my leadership team and in they came; one by one; led by Andrew, who was fussing around them, being sycophantic and out of character.

They made themselves coffees and sat opposite us at the long board room table. We had the heads of Quality, Finance, HR, Sales and Continuous Improvement. Not quite the grown-ups, (the Americans) but certainly the adolescents of the business.

After several minutes of inane chatter and complaining about the traveling they all had endured to arrive at our plant, Andrew addressed the whole room.

'Thank you all for coming. I thought it would be worthwhile to let you know what the current situation with the plant performance is here. We will also address the purpose of the impending visit from Mr. Roger Rewinkle, the President of the Global group.' Andrew paused for effect, looking around the room before continuing.

'As you know we have engaged Frank Walsh…' he catches my eye and pauses as all eyes are on me. … 'here to step into the breach as General Manager while we find the right candidate. The point made many times is that we have had three General Managers in as many years. It's unsettling and we need to find the right candidate, so, if I can ask Frank to give us his initial thoughts and ideas going forward.'

This was a surprise to me as there was no mention of what this agenda was going to be, despite the fact that I had asked Andrew several times for one so I could prepare! I wondered, not for the first time if the fox in the room was right here today.

Andrew appeared oblivious to my surprise and continued, 'As you know, we are in our second quarter of the fiscal year and we will be declaring a loss year to date. We need to demonstrate to the owners what we are going to do to recover the situation in the remaining eight months that are left.' Again, he paused, I knew what he was doing, and I waited for the question.

'Frank can I ask what your view is?'

'Well, the team are focused and capable now but they need more time to help support the plant.'

Andrew looked bemused; 'What are you suggesting?'

He had provoked me and it was time to hit back hard. I leaned forward on the table looking at the all the executive leadership team.

'I'm proposing a lockdown.' Now I paused, for effect.

'Lockdown?' Andrew asked. Interestingly, we had all been in the room for at least twenty minutes and the only voice we were all hearing was Andrew. Never surround yourself with people who do not contribute.

'Yes, it's a penal term. Lockdown; stop everything you are doing as a natural part of your day until what you have is back under control.' I continued, 'I have been here now for four weeks. I have not had a full squad of my team present at any one time; the reason being that despite the fact we are in recovery mode you are all treating the plant as though it's business as usual, a normal working condition which blatantly it is not. Each of you have demanded or ordered one of my team at some point to attend days off site or conference calls that last most of the day because that's how you all run the other plants.'

Silence!

I sat back, 'Well how's that working out for you?'

The team were incredulous with that statement. However, it was the truth. Matrix management only works if you have the bigger picture in your head, not the blinkered view of your own department or domain.

Andrew spoke. 'How do you mean? Give us an example.'

'Sarah, for example, she was off for three days last week to attend a conference on a new hygiene programme because we want to get a recognized nationwide accreditation.'

'And?' Andrew challenged.

'Well, she is not at the plant ensuring we can recover the situation while she is attaining an accreditation which, quite frankly, we are very far away from attaining. It is a waste of everyone else's time.'

I went on; 'Stuart in finance; he spends hours of his time putting together a PowerPoint pack of some eighty odd slides to satisfy the needs of Group Finance. He is not doing the forensic finance for this plant that I know he loves to do and that I desperately need: we never see the guy.' I smiled at Stuart but he looked mortified.

The senior team furtively looked at each other as if to acknowledge the truth. Andrew asked for the truth so he was going to get it. I continued, 'To compound it all, when we review the presentation, he so painstakingly put together we're lucky to get past slide six, let alone the eighty-nine the poor man had to produce for you lot!' Stuart looked like he was going to cry.

I was met with silence.

'As for Sales,' I continued, really getting into my stride, 'customers are leaving us in droves and we have downgraded our forecast; yet we expect Mark to spend a week away from the business with the central sales team at a conference about where we are going in the future? If this continues there will be no future,' I declared. Mark nodded.

'So, lockdown means no one from outside coming in and no one from the plant going outside until I have this plant under control.' This time I was met with shock.

Eventually Didier, the French financial director of the European group spoke.

'But Frank, we need information; we are here to help.'

'Didier, I appreciate you need information but I do not see how the executive leadership team is helping by taking away valuable resources to meet their own needs.'

Didier was taken back. I don't think he had ever been addressed in this manner. 'But I am expecting to see the full recovery plan for this site today so we can analysis it before we present it to Roger and the team next week.'

You could hear the gasps of surprise and see the incredulous faces of my team. Where did this come from?

Didier continued, 'We sent out notification of this six weeks ago!'

Considering I had only been in the Plant four weeks I had no answer so I looked directly at Andrew. He spoke, his earlier bravado was missing and he wouldn't look me in the eye. 'Yes, we need to present the recovery plan to the owners on Monday.' I looked around the room, shaking my head and Didier spoke next.

'I was expecting to review it today; I thought that was the purpose of the meeting here today?'

The team slumped in their chairs, we were not prepared because we hadn't been asked or given enough notice. We were led to believe the purpose of the meeting was to agree the agenda for the state visit. It was becoming clear that the executive senior team were actually part of the problem.

Didier continued, 'Due to the lack of time we will need a conference call to prepare for the presentation sometime before their arrival on Monday morning.'

'Well, it's Tuesday now,' I said. 'Are you expecting this team to come up with a recovery plan in three days?'

'Yes, we need this information; we gave you six weeks' notice to come up with a recovery plan. We must have a conference call this Sunday,' Didier insisted. Gasps from my team.

I didn't hesitate.

'No!' I exclaimed. 'Neither I, nor any of my team will spend their precious Sunday on a conference call to satisfy your requirements, considering we have only just been made aware of the circumstances.' I glared at Andrew; he wasn't so talkative now.

Now I knew what it was like to be thrown under a bus!

I had nothing else to say. Silence is a great tool if used correctly and proportionately. *

What ensued was a debacle; the executive leadership team started arguing amongst themselves.

Eventually the Frenchman lost his patience. Didier held his hand up and stated in his strong French accent: 'I have had enough! Enough!' He stood up and left the room.

I interrupted the silence, 'clearly he likes his eggs!'

I smiled and left the boardroom with my team in silence, we were in a state shock. In the reception area I turned to them, 'C'mon team let me buy you all a coffee.' I gestured to the canteen.

The atmosphere was solemn and the air filled with anxiety. I knew as a leader I had to diffuse the situation and get them all focused on the job in hand. It was clear we would have to come up with the recovery plan because the Executive leadership team simply was not capable. As I handed out the coffees to everyone, I made reassuring comments. I could see for the first time they were all grateful to have a leader that would stand up for them. Respect is earned and I think I cemented it that day when I declared that none of my team would be attending any conference call in the precious time they should be spending with their families. We work to live.

I sat a while with the team in the canteen trying to reassure everyone. I could sense some were thinking they needed to polish their CV's. I was thinking… how do we come up with a recovery plan in three days?

Later that day….

Five o'clock came and I shut down my computer. As I clocked out, I popped my head into HR to find Paula the HR manager there.

'Any plans tonight?' I enquired.

'None,' Paula said.

'Fancy a bite to eat at the hotel?' We both worked away from home.

'Sure, why not! Nothing else planned.'

I smiled, 'bring your note pad; we've got work to do.'

There's no such thing as a free meal in these dark days, but I needed help; a sounding board. 'Shall we say 7pm in the bar?' Paula agreed and I picked up my bag to head to my hotel.

I headed for the car park. My attention was caught by the fact the lights in Daniel's office were still on. It concerned me that he was working past the clocking out time. I know we were in difficulty but we had to be refreshed every night to come into work the next day revitalized and not tired. I went to his office.

'What time do you call this?' I enquired. 'Daniel, always leaves work on time.'

'I know, I know; you said before.'

'I need you alert and fit for what tomorrow throws at you. Remember, you can only change what's in your sphere of influence.'

I sat down. Daniel joined me and I opened up to him.

'My father died recently; he was only young and he worked all his life but he worked too long hours; and for what?' Daniel was unsure how to respond so I continued, 'work is a never-ending process; it's a fact and we may as well get used to it, therefore stop focusing on 1 day or 1 week and start planning for a career. Harness the skills of time management and stop trying to get everything done in a day.' Daniel nodded.

'I remember a manager of mine came to me almost in tears, telling me "I can't do all this; I'm struggling," to which I replied, "Rome wasn't built in a day". He retorted, "Only because you aren't in charge Frank!"'

Daniel laughed; he was a little more relaxed. I didn't want him thinking I was blowing my own trumpet but that I wanted to support him through this rough time.

'The company you work for is important but so is your family, infinitely more so than any job. Family*will always enrich your life more than a company ever can so give them the time they deserve.'

'If you fall in life neither the company you work for nor your boss will lend you a helping hand; your family will. Don't get me wrong I used to be conflicted with this. I try to be a good boss and always try to be there for my staff, but families – they will always be there, no questions asked.

Work would drop you in a heartbeat if they felt it would benefit the bottom line. Life is not only about work, office, and the company - I love the people and the industry I work in, and when we socialize it's fantastic, but do you know what? That's one moment. With friends and family, it's everlasting and unconditional. Cherish your moments with family and friends.' I went on, almost fatherly in my approach. 'I was the son of a father I rarely saw due to work and I've seen families torn apart because parents put work before family. I've heard of young fathers passing away because of stress at work and people working 16 hours a day'

'Listen to me Daniel. A person who stays late at the office is not a hardworking person. I understand why people would disagree but I have a different view. I have learnt in 20 years of working at all different levels that those who are able to work effectively in the time provided are hugely successful and enjoy a great work life balance. If you are working 10-12 hours, I beg you to look at what you are trying achieve and question whether you are genuinely adding benefit.' Daniel nodding, listened intently.

I spoke softly now 'Plan your day before you start it, don't do it at 8am or 8.30am after your day has started as you're already chasing your tail. Don't be a busy fool. You did not study hard or struggle in life to become a machine, did you?'

'No, no I didn't.'

'With the right fuel machines can operate 24 hours a day. You cannot. Balance your life. Remember you have 24 hours in a day; 8 hours to sleep; 8 hours to work and 8 hours of your own. I'm going to teach you something about how precious time is later. If I have to ask anyone to work late or work late myself, I am a fool. To date, I have never asked anyone to work late and I never will. There's more to life than working late,' I declared. Practice what you preach!

'You're right.' expressed Daniel. I stood up.

'C'mon, I'll buy you something stronger than a coffee.' Daniel smiled, stood up, and we both left for the night. It was five thirty-five.

(C)John Paul Reeves, 2011

CHAPTER 11

HR Jenga

Paula was dutifully waiting for me at the restaurant table. She smiled as I entered the room and I walked over to her.

'Thanks for waiting.'

'Pleasure,' she said.

'What's good here?' I asked looking at the menu.

'It's all good: I've eaten the menu three times over,' she laughed.

'Well, what would you recommend?'

'The duck is usually cooked to perfection.'

'Duck it is then.' I placed the menu down and took a folded piece of A4 paper from my pocket and handed it over. She took it and started to unravel it.

The waiter came and went with our order. Paula read the paper which was a list of twelve names. She studied it intently then looked at me?

'Well certainly a gallery of rogues here!' she exclaimed. I was glad she said that.

'What's the ratio between the Direct and the In-direct?'

'What do you mean?'

'Well, in the Direct headcount is an operator who is hands-on in the process and materials, he actually produces something. His cost is all in the Cost of Sales which forms part of the Sales Price. Take one from the other and we end up with a Gross Margin for the product.' She nodded. 'An In-direct worker has a support function to the operation but actually does not produce anything apart from reports.'

She smiled and nodded. 'Yes, I know all about that.' Another reference to the group HR Director, I suspected.

'People wearing ties cost me money, people without ties make me money.' She nodded as she recognized the comparisons.

'The average full cost of Direct is around £28k per year. The average full cost of In-direct is £38k per year. A 10k difference.'

'Yes, I see,' Paula said.

'Do you know the ratio between direct to indirect staff?'

'No sorry, but I guess I should know.'

'It is 55% direct to 45% indirect. It's far too high. We need to get to 70% Direct to 30% Indirect. This will give us more people on the factory floor making product and 30% supporting them.'

'I see, if that was the case, we would save around £300k annualized on salaries alone.'

'So, over the last two weeks I have been doing one to ones with all the In-directs; shadowing them and understanding what they contribute. I have come up with a list on which I would like your opinion.'

'Sure, where do you want to start?'

'Well, let's call this operation Jenga.'

'Jenga?' Paula enquired.

'Yes, the game of Jenga is a tower of bricks intertwined. You carefully remove one brick at a time making sure the whole structure doesn't collapse. It's surprising how many building bricks you can take out while the structure still remains intact.' I nodded to the piece of paper, 'however, the skill is to ensure that you don't take the wrong brick out. Should you remove one important brick from the structure, then it would all collapse?' Paula nodded. 'That's why I need your expertise and guidance on this. Be mindful that this will all happen on one day. We will dismiss the right people, then no others. There's enough uncertainty as it is.'

The waiter brought our drinks and I took a sip from my glass, thinking for a moment. 'Sometimes, Paula, the more people you have in layers of management positions the more the structure becomes convoluted. Blockers between departments begin to form and it stops progress. What we need to do here is to move swiftly on, regaining profitability to the business, otherwise instead of eleven people going, it could be the whole site. That's nearly two hundred and fifty people.'

'Yes,' Paula looked very serious. 'I do understand. Operation Jenga it is!'

In the next 90 minutes between courses, we discussed and debated each individual name on the list, their functions; their performances and their contribution. It was a healthy debate. Paula was made to feel an equal. The neutral and informal setting really helped her open up and allowed her to feel free to disagree with some of my assumptions. We concluded the dinner and interestingly of all the names I had on the list she only disagreed with one: More about him later.

The other eleven would be earmarked for removal from the business. These were In-directs brought on board due to the poor implementation of the ERP system. It was clear this was the business's answer to the problem. Throw very expensive bodies at it. I had a different view on ERP which I was going to share with the Vice President of IT for the Group. He was called Bob Border and he was part of the USA visiting team next Monday.

I want to be clear here, my definition of LEAN deviates slightly from the well-known quote from Dr Dan Jones. 'Lean is doing twice as much, in half the space, with half the people.' My quote differs - the beginning is the same but I conclude, "with the same people." I don't care much for focus on headcount reduction; I think the business making more money, more effectively, with happy customers should be the focus.

When you start the journey of implementing LEAN you have to be very clear that no one will be terminated by any improvements that LEAN activities will bring.

Therefore, evaluate your team and remove those you feel are surplus at that time, because once you start making the improvements no-one can be seen as a casualty of LEAN initiatives. If they are, LEAN will fail and so will your business.

CHAPTER 12

A Team Effort

The next day was business as usual; if we could call it that in those troubled times. I had a plan and I needed to begin executing it. Remembering not to have a meeting with my team before two pm, I called them all in at three o'clock. Why 2pm? A recent study of bio-rhythms showed that although each individual has a personal rhythm there are numerous similarities between all humans - The 'efficiency curve'.

The study's conclusion was that maximum productivity is achieved around 10 am in the morning. This is not attained at any other time of the day whatever we may think. After lunch the efficiency curve gets very low indeed; however, there is a slight surge towards the end of the afternoon, (as we can see the finishing line ahead of us, we naturally sprint).

Therefore, your most productive time is the morning so don't waste it in meetings. Clearly there are exceptions but, in my view, only for customers, which brings me to my next point. Unnecessary meetings.

A recent study conducted in America of 300 managers on an average salary of $50,000 showed that they spent half their time in meetings.

Add up the hourly salaries of each of your colleagues and multiply by the time spent in the meeting. Also add in travelling costs, time lost on conversation and coffee breaks!

Doctors, solicitors, and psychiatrists, oh, and dare I say it? consultants… In all cases their performance is remunerated in the time they spend with their clients. Why not the management of an organization?

Remember time is money, so with every minute you are costing money.

Also, punctuality used to be an expression of integrity and respect for each other's position and time. Regrettably, punctuality has in my opinion drifted and an almost casual approach to attending meetings on time has become ubiquitous.

One good way to measure time wasted and put a cost to it is this: 8 people wait 5 minutes 8 x 5 = 40mins. Discount*the obvious disrespect the person has shown to the individuals kept waiting, now work out the cost to the company 40 minutes x your company hourly rate.

Once you've set the precedent on when a meeting should take place and that you should be punctual, then set the agenda!

Agenda is simple:

What is the aim of the meeting?

What is the objective of the meeting?

Define it, display it and very importantly, set the deadline.

The more verbose amongst us tend to lead the meeting and want to hear only their own voice.

A meeting should last no longer than an hour. Studies have shown that a person's attention waivers after an hour. Be strict and be challenging. After all, if you define the business in a ten-minute meeting every morning, then an hour should be ample time to solve the big issues of the day?

One senior executive used to have a bucket full of sponge balls and every time you digressed away from the subject, he would throw a ball at you! Another used to put an egg timer on his desk when the meeting started and set it for an hour. When it went off loudly, he would leave the meeting even if you were in full flow knee deep in sponge balls!

(C)John Paul Reeves, 2011

So, back to my current troubleshooting. My team gathered on time; they looked slightly uneasy at this impromptu call as I had broken my number 1 rule - set an agenda. Sometimes it is necessary to break the rules for the greater good. I opened the meeting standing at the white board.

'Why is time so important? Imagine that you won a competition and your prize was the transfer of £86,400 into your personal bank account every morning for your own use. However, there are rules.'

They all smiled relaxing into where I was taking the exercise.

'Everything you didn't spend during the day would be taken away from you. You may not simply transfer money into some other account, you may only spend it.'

Some of the teams were scribbling the rules down in excitement.

'The second rule is the bank can end the game at any time without warning. It can also close the account and you will not receive a new one.' This rule threw them a bit so I threw them the bait.

'So, my question is, what you would personally do?'

Mark was the first to speak. 'You would buy everything you desired, not only for yourself but for your family and friends, even strangers as you couldn't spend it all on yourself at any time, could you?' They all nodded in agreement.

'We still have to work I guess?' asked Graham, the engineering manager.

'Yes,' I replied and what ensued was a healthy debate about what to spend money on when you haven't got the time to think about it.

'If you haven't worked it out, the sum of £86400 represents the number of seconds in a day'. *Sighs from around the room. 'The magical bank account is time and what we haven't lived up to for the day is lost and gone forever. These seconds are worth so much more than money; enjoy every second of your life because time races by so much more quickly than you think and we are a long time dead!' I recognize the look of dawning realization on the faces around the room.

I wrote up the following on the board: The priority quad.

	Urgent	**Not Urgent**
Important	• Breakdowns • Accidents • Real targets	• Research • Benchmarking • Thinking • Learning
Not Important	• Meetings • E Mails • Phonecalls • False targets •Reports	• Idle chat •Gossip

"Now, put in a working week a percentage factor you think you spend your time on as a manager. They all furiously jotted down their idea of where their time was going. I concluded.

'Sixty per cent of your time is spent on the urgent, but not important. Remember the "you must have that report done for today!" Something that already happened a month ago! Why are you not dealing with the urgent issue of the day? Stuart?' I picked him out, but Stuart, the finance controller nodded furiously in agreement.

<table>
<tr><td></td><td>Urgent</td><td>Not Urgent</td></tr>
<tr><td>Important</td><td>• Breakdowns
• Accidents
• Real targets
25%</td><td>• Research
• Benchmarking
• Thinking
• Learning
10%</td></tr>
<tr><td>Not Important</td><td>• Meetings
• E Mails
• Phonecalls
• False targets
•Reports 60%</td><td>• Idle chat
•Gossip
5%</td></tr>
</table>

'Here's where world class managers should really be; 5% on emails and meetings. 20% on actually doing. 60% on learning, teaching and benchmarking.' I completed the quad on the board and my team acknowledge the difference in their time control.

	Urgent	**Not Urgent**
Important	• Breakdowns • Accidents • Real targets **20%**	• Research • Benchmarking • Thinking • Learning **65%**
Not Important	• Meetings • E Mails • Phonecalls • False targets •Reports **15%**	• Idle chat •Gossip **0%**

'So How much time do we really have?' I asked. 'Team, follow me on this and I want you all to do a formula sum at the end of it.' I turned to the board and I wrote on it:

8 hours to sleep

2 hours to eat

1 hour for personal hygiene

8 hours working

1 hour transport

Sarah piped up, 'That's 20 hours in total,' she exclaimed proudly.

'Correct. So then 20 hours accounted for only leaves us 4 hours to live.' A realization came over the team and I continued:

'We are led to believe that three score years and ten is the average lifespan, although that's increased in recent years, but even so, thank goodness for weekends!" They all smiled and I continued:

'We are awake 16 hours per day. We watch TV 20 hours per week, maybe? So that equals 65 days in a calendar year,' I continued to write on the board and looked around to add, 'we know there are 365 days per year? Yes?'

They all agreed.

'We work 46 weeks per year?' Yes again.

'We work 5 days per week; 46 weeks in the year multiplied by 5 days per week = 230 working days per year.' They were listening intently now.

'So, if we take the total days per year minus the days we have work, we are left with?'

Stuart was first to come up with the answer. Well, I'd hope so. After all he is the financial controller.

'135 days,' he announced proudly. So, I summarized my calculation:

'We know we have non-Free Time of 20 hours; that's working, travelling, hygiene, eating etc.? We on average watch TV 24 hours per week, which is equal to 65 days per year!' I continued to scribble on the board.

'Let's assume we all, on average, live the biblical amount of time of three score years and ten; 70 years to live.'

I began to write the formula on the board.

65 days per year left for you at 3 score and 10 (70x65 days left for you) – Your current Age (x 65)

'How many days left do you have for yourself ? * Do you actually have to live?'

I stopped and turned. They all started to calculate. The realization dawned on each and every one of them.

'There are not many days left for you are there?' As the fact dawned on all of them, I turned and I did my own calculation on the board.

'I'm fifty-four,' some gasped as they thought I was much older I guess: I lightened the mood by adding, 'I had two paper rounds and they were both up hills.' The silence was broken by some laughter.

'So, 70 minus my age 54 equals 16 x 65 days left for myself = 1040 days left!' I put down the pen and looked around the room, 'and I'm spending this day with you! So, time is more precious than you give it credit for.' They all nodded in agreement.

I concluded, 'hopefully I've convinced you that time is money and also the most valuable thing you have personally.' They all nodded 'Remember, time is the only coin of your life. It is the only coin you have and only you can determine how it will be spent. Be careful lest you let other people spend it for you.'

Next, I turned to the business at hand bringing the team back to reality with a renewed focus, or so I hoped. 'So, the recovery plan for the grownups on Monday? Any ideas? Use your time wisely.' I looked around the room. The task was daunting to try and compile something with credence in such a short period of time. I sensed the team was lost so I wanted to exorcise their frustrations. I made a provocative comment to release the tension.

'So how do you think we got into this situation?'

'Because they didn't do their job properly!' exclaimed Mark glaring at Scott. I knew he would be the first and this opened up the floodgates.

'They rushed that ERP implementation and now we are left holding the baby,' exclaimed Sarah. 'It's a stock nightmare out there, we still don't know how much WIP we have and we cannot keep promising what we can't deliver.'

Scott waded in. 'Hang on a minute, we have a schedule; we only make what we are told.'

'Bullshit!!' Mark butted in; his usual demeanour gone; he was clearly angry. 'You make what you think we need, not what we tell you to.' I stepped in before it went too far.

'Gentlemen, please!'

'Remember, none of us comes to work to be spoken to like that, Mark. You have a warning; no more please.' I soften, 'we have to work together, this isn't working together, and fighting now won't solve any issues. We have our 5-day plan remember. This is open forum time so come on, be honest but polite.' Silence!

'The enemy is outside in the marketplace, our competitors taking our customers. The enemy is not right here, right now,' I continued.

I listened intently. Remember; two ears one mouth.

'Where are they all now? They're the ones that caused the bloody mess in the first place,' Graeme declared. 'They should tell us what their plans are to fix it.'

'Who are they?' Scott again. 'Who made the decision to use this crappy system?'

'We can't blame the system, Scott,' Mark interrupted, 'it's the lack of training and understanding from Operations which is hindering everything. You made the decision to go live.'

Scott shook his head, speechless at Mark's accusations.

'Andrew was the one who made the call,' Stuart this time; his voice was quiet and everyone stopped talking. 'I told him we weren't ready but he overruled it; I kept telling him this would happen but he never listened!'

I stored this information up; there are always two sides to every story but privately I was starting to see Andrew for the fox he was. I would deal with him when the time came.

I continued to listen intently. Remember, two ears one mouth.

'Will they close us if we don't turn it around?' asked Daniel. The room went silent and they all stared at me for reassurance.

'Well, let me tell you something; John Harvey Jones was the CBI President and he famously made a quote which is very profound: "The purpose of any organization is to create wealth for its shareholders and owners; it is not to provide jobs or long-term careers. It's wealth, pure and simple." They all listened. 'If it was your money invested and we were going to lose two million pounds a year why would you continue? It would be madness, right?' Most nodded in agreement.

'Are we really that close?' asked Scott, a flicker of worry in his eyes.

'Scott, we are where we are! I always say if you point a finger there will be three pointing back.' I gestured with my finger to show them. 'We are the team that will pull it around; we are the only team that knows how to pull it around,' I stood up and cleared the board.

'Let's approach this as if we are reading a P and L sheet. Let's start with sales.' I drew a graph then added April through to December on it.

'Next let's look at the cost of sales. So that's everything we need to pay out to make the product. We have fixed costs such as rent, heating, lighting etc. so, we should only look at the variable costs.'

'Variable costs?' asked Daniel.

'Yes, variable, like overtime. Costs which are different every month - temporary staff, and the big one of course - waste!'

'Then there's staff.' The room fell silent. I turned to observe for a moment and they all looked uneasy except Paula who had already done her homework.

'So, Paula what did we come up with?' They all turned to Paula who had her book open in front of her.

'Well, with the people we've identified we would save £224k this fiscal year if we enacted the removals by next Friday.' The rest of the team were surprised. 'That would be £300k annualized next year.'

'Thank you, Paula.'

'Which names?' enquired Mark, asking the question on everyone's mind.

I went to the laptop and displayed on the screen the names and departments where the losses would occur.

'Who came up with these names?' Asked Daniel.

'I did!' I replied. The team looked intently at the names.

Graham piped up, 'Well, I wouldn't miss any of them!'

'I know this is tough but we need to cut the finger off to save the hand, not wait until we have to remove the whole arm,' I said. 'All these will be dealt with fairly and will get over the odds to recompense.'

I waited for a confrontation on any of the names but none came. I had done my due diligence well.

I took the list down; Paula and I would deal with them all next Friday.

'Next big cost: waste!' I wrote on the board. 'Scott what's the current wastage monthly.'

'We are running at around 24%.' Gasps from the room.

'Stuart, what's the financial impact of 1% waste to the bottom line?'

'Around £20k.' Another gasp. It's amazing how the senior team only know their important numbers for their departments and not that of the whole business.

'So, 24 x £20k is £480k.' When you write hard facts on the board it's amazing how it focuses their minds. 'Look, even if we aim to eliminate 1% of waste per month over 12 months, we would get £240k back.'

'Remember, the deficit is 2 million and with the two initiatives that we can control we get back £420k.'

I turned to Mark, 'now Sales.'

Mark shuffled in his seat. 'Well, we've got several opportunities which I am confident of, but can they be delivered?' Mark looked at Scott and Daniel.

'Yes!' I said confidently and we worked through some of the detail behind the sales forecast.

When we completed the meeting (within the hour) we had clawed back the deficit to an end of year figure of minus £600k. I was happy with that as the foundations would have been laid for the following year to build upon. We estimated that we could save £1.4m.

Who wouldn't be happy with that? Now all we had to do was deliver the recovery plan.

Stuart and I then went about putting it into a format that was easily understandable as I was going to present it to the Americans when they arrived on Monday.

It was a simple four slide summary.

Slide one was current position.

Slide two was a spreadsheet showing the initiatives throughout the remaining part of the year and the money it would generate.

Slide three was a sales summary of the extra revenue we would generate.

Slide four was the things we wanted help with from them.

This would be a contentious debate, no doubt, but I always believe the grown-ups should be part of the solution as well. We needed extra cash for machinery and direct staff so I was interested to see what they would say.

First, I needed to run the whole thing past Andrew. I wasn't happy with Andrew. My head and gut told me he was a terrible decision maker and good at trying to hide his mistakes too. However, I knew I needed to tread carefully here as he was also a fox who could bite if pushed. I arranged a meeting and sent him the deck for review.

A meeting invite appeared two hours later and the next morning I found myself sitting in his office running through the plan.

'Do you think you can do it?' Andrew asked.

'Yes: I believe we can.'

Andrew stared at the spreadsheet. 'Well, that would be a hell of an achievement if you could pull it off,' he said, doubtfully.

'Yes, I'm confident in the numbers, we've got a good team here.'

'All this without touching the ERP system?'

'Yes, you see the ERP system is functionally working at the moment. We can get finance reports out of it, we can raise dispatch notes and invoices.'

'What about the improvements Frank? We need to get the system working more efficiently. We've invested a fortune in the work and it's far from finished.'

I lifted my phone from my pocket. 'Andrew this phone has 320 functions and I only use four. Emails, phone calls, text messaging and internet. That's all I need it for. It's fit for function.'

I continued, I needed to see his response.

'The ERP system has thousands of applications and would like to haves. We just need it functional. We've over complicated it and as a result, generated extra work using very expensive bodies who in turn made it more complicated.' Andrew nodded in agreement but I could see he was far from convinced. 'Look, my suggestion is we remove the unnecessary costs we are carrying with all the iterations they are thinking of making to the system. We must stop the releases for 6 months while we stabilize delivery. On-time delivery has made a step change improvement since we rolled out the red-hot list from our sales colleagues. Confidence is slowly growing within the team and now we have a recovery plan to back it up.'

'What help do you need from me?' Andrew inquired.

'Stop the IT department from making their changes and let's just get back to a steady state.'

'That's a major ask Frank.' Andrew looked perturbed but reluctantly agreed so I carried on to my next point before he had a chance to reconsider.

'We have issues with a major customer and we cannot afford to have any nasty surprises from production. Mark has asked me to go and see the customer with him; persuade them not to pull out.'

'Yes, I know the customer; £7 million account.' Andrew sighed and he looked resigned to the fact they were going to leave us. I almost felt sorry for him until he spoke. 'What can you possibly do to fix this then Frank?'

'Well, I'd like to offer them an alternative to stay?'

'They have formally written to us about withdrawing; what could you possibly do?' Andrew enquired, the negativity and disbelief evident in his tone.

'Well, I'd like to offer them a 5% discount right now. Then I would ask them to allow two of their engineers to join us for a two-week period here at the plant for a kaizen event.'

'Kaizen event?'

'Yes, it's a week-long event with a cross functional team consisting of around 10 to 12 people. We would use kaizen methodology. Put into place a system whereby we would deliver 100 % on time and take out 5% of the cost of the product to compensate for the reduction.'

Andrew sat thoughtful in silence. I continued, 'Look Andrew, this is a golden opportunity for us. We can demonstrate to the two engineers the improvements they will see by the end of the week as well as the effort we are all putting in to overcoming the problem.'

'I'm not sure;' he was on the defensive; I could sense it. What was he hiding?

'Sorry, I don't understand? I am offering to save this customer. You should be behind the team, Andrew.' I tried to soften my voice but I was feeling the hostility. 'A customer will always remember how you overcame a problem long after the problem has been forgotten,' I declared.

'I just don't want to cause anymore disruption, we had….' He faltered, either trying to cover his tracks or this time he was being honest. 'I had some uncomfortable conversations with that customer during the ERP implementation. They had experienced similar problems with the same system. They advised us not to go ahead.' He broke eye contact, 'but we did it anyway.'

'We?' I challenged his reply, 'who gave the go-ahead Andrew?' He didn't reply, just deflected, 'When are you meeting with them?' he enquired.

'Tomorrow.'

Andrew looked surprised.

'Mark has arranged it. I have all the facts, and we are delivering around 65% on time with an 8% reject rate.'

'So, you did this without checking with me first and you now believe that through this "kaizen event" you are going to deliver 100% on time with zero defects?'

His emphasis on "kaizen event" irritated me. In fact, his whole attitude was hostile but I rose above it. In my opinion a mistake made should be brought to the surface not covered by layers of nonsense which others have to work through. It's devious and unnecessary.

'Yes.' That's all the response he was getting from me now. It was time to take control of this mess with, or without Andrew's blessing.

'Well good luck with that!'

I smiled and left the room. Andrew needed to leave this business. He was actively blocking progress and it wasn't helping morale but I needed to play him at his own game, which I would. I need to keep my mind focused on the upcoming kaizen event plans. Kaizen blitz is a good way of focusing the mind on a single problem. With the right facilitation kaizen can work wonders in step change results. All I had to do now was deliver it. Success is the best form of revenge and I needed to show Andrew what his team was capable of.

CHAPTER 13

Last Chance Saloon

The next morning Mark and I headed to his car ready to see the customer, Mark was driving.

'Thanks for coming with me Frank.'

'No problem; always good to support my colleagues.'

'Well, yes, but you're the first General Manager to do so in all the times I've had to go and see disgruntled customers.'

'Hasn't Andrew been with you?'

Mark scoffed, 'not once has he even offered; sits in his office hoping things will eventually change for the better.'

I thought that very strange; clearly no support for the troops in the firing line from the very top.

'Well, at least they now have a target apart from you to have a go at.' We both smiled. 'Talk through the people Mark; tell me who we are to be dealing with today.'

'There's Nigel, he is the Procurement Director, and then there's Jean-Luc, the Managing Director.'

'OK.'

'We've really pissed them off big time.'

'So, I gather.' We drove in silence for a moment.

'So, what is this kaizen event?' enquired Mark, changing the subject.

I started to explain.

'Mark, I believe that now we have identified the need for change, and how we can manage our time more effectively to help those changes we need to make. So how do we do it? This is the next stage. We need a plan or roadmap to follow to ensure it can be sustained, Kaizen is the favoured model. First, though, we need to go to the Gemba.'

'Gemba?' asked Mark.

'Gemba is where the work is done; where the money is made, or even lost. On this foundation stone we can build a culture of the 3 kaizen principles with the 7 concepts. On these foundations we lay the first 5S-Visual Management-People Involvement. What happens to a building without any foundation stones?'

'Well, it collapses, I guess,' Mark answered.

'Exactly!' I went on to explain the principles and concepts of kaizen methodology. It was a good thing the journey would take several hours as there was a lot to go through.

'Each business in their eager pursuit of Quality, Cost, Delivery and Profitability run with "Total Production Management (TPM) combined with "Total Quality Management" (TQM) and strive for "Just in Time" (JIT) to try and achieve these honourable goals. However, without the culture of the foundation stones it will simply struggle.'

'OK, I get that,' said Mark.

The "Gemba" is where the real value-creating work actually occurs. The depth of the exploitation of its value to managers and leaders is often missed. It requires a trained Manager at every level who understands that opportunities and issues can be spotted by just observing day to day operations. When a problem occurs, you will notice there isn't the slightest notion of sitting down in a room to talk over the problem. How can you talk through a problem when you are sat down in a room away from the issues? Instead, they instantly stride to the location of the problem – the Gemba – along with whoever else should be with them.

They do this because they know that the data they find will be fresh and in its 'natural state' – and it is seen by everyone involved at the same time… before the stories begin to be spun. The leaders, the experienced ones, know the rich value of immediate interaction with the employees as it provides them with practical information. This information is coming from operators who may well know best. Remember the iceberg of ignorance?'

Mark nodded, keeping his eyes on the road but listening.

'In addition, these leaders also know the positive impact on the employees –when it is done right. When the operators see management is really interested and their pursuit of the data needed to solve the problem is genuine, they should step up and support. In other words, when managers approach the Gemba with respect and a positive attitude of, "What can we learn from this situation and improve upon?" and "What can I do to help the operations folks make their jobs easier?" Good things can happen. Positive, supportive, and genuine exchanges which take place at the Gemba can reinforce the employees' self-image and, build a feeling of genuine engagement that they are doing meaningful work. It is essential that this is verified by the management and by the way that they are responding. Such positive interactions are part of a manager's responsibility. They just need training.'

'So, it's a lot about moral and empowerment?' asked Mark.

"Treating people with respect and valuing their opinion provides clear evidence to them that managers and employees are equally valued members of a professional team. This shows understanding of what collaboration means in generating results which are substantial and sustainable.'

'Well, that would go a long way with the Henderson survey,' Mark declared.

'Henderson survey?' I asked.

'Yes, it's the annual employee survey. The States places a lot of credence on it. It's a survey given to everyone from manager's staff to shop floor.'

'Interesting!'

'Yes, so it's all done electronically and anonymously.'

'OK!'

'Last year's score was 22 points out of a possible 100.'

'Wow!'

'Yes, we are the worst performing plant in the global footprint.'

One to tackle later, I noted.

'Well, we can change this Mark; our kaizen event will cascade change across the business. The first step of the kaizen principles is relevant to this,' I continued, 'measure Trends not Results.'

'Never go for the result only. You know this Mark, in Sales terms you could be the best salesman in one month and the worst in the next, measure trends of improvement in all areas.'

'Yes, tell me about it! Worst thing about working in Sales,' scoffed Mark.

'Indeed!' I smile and continued, 'so, Kaizen Principle 2. Speak with data, not opinion: Always speak with informed data to make those important decisions. Emotion evokes emotion.

'If I said Manchester United is the most successful football team in history that may cause a little emotion.'

'Bloody right it would!'

I laughed; I knew Mark was a Leeds supporter.

'But Mark, in fact the statistics or the data clearly puts Liverpool as the most successful club in history.'

'Are you trying to raise my blood pressure even more before this meeting Frank? What about the third principle then?'

'Kaizen Principle 3 is to be non-blaming, non-judgmental. Remember if you are pointing fingers at anyone there's always three pointing back at you. You have got to create the environment where people are readily accepting of failure and are able to let you know.'

So now we have the three principles of kaizen that are supported by the seven concepts.

'Go on then' Mark prompted. 'What are the seven concepts?'

I started to reel them off.

'Kaizen Concept 1. Customer Driven - Customer First.' Mark was happy with that one.

'Kaizen Concept 2. Root Cause analysis looks beyond the trees, even below you. Problems happen! It's how we make sure they never happen, again and you do this by eliminating the root cause.'

'Kaizen Concept 3. Customer quality. Whether they be internal in your organization, or your supplier, and especially your customer; never move anything on to the next stage if it's deficit in any way.

"Kaizen Concept 4. Speak with Data. It's also one of the key principles.'

'Kaizen Concept 5. Upstream Management not Top Down. If it comes from bottom up it will be sustaining.

Like if we introduced Six Sigma to the shop floor. It's all Greek to them.'

Mark laughed!

'Top down initiitives are always seen to be elitist and never get down to the root causes. Kaizen gets to the shop floor, or the gemba, quicker and that's where you find the solutions to our problems. Not from some statastician.'

'Kaizen Concept 6. Plan, Do. Check, Act, turns to a Standard. Plan, Do, Check, Act, equals higher standards.'

Mark nodded.

'But then we must do SDCA standardize, do, check it again, act, if the standard needs upgrading. Like the current standard has been used for decades because that's the way the machine should be set up. Why can't it be improved to a higher standard?'

'Kaizen Concept 7. Celebrate Achievements and Recognize Rewards. That's so important for morale. One of the key things I learnt as a manager is, I am responsible for providing the 5 M's. If I provide all these then there would not be any reason for me to point any fingers at anyone. I, as a manager, declare that I will provide my workforce to the best of my ability these 5M standards.'

'Go on then.' Interrupted Mark. 'What are the 5M's?'

'Means, Methods, Material, Machine and Manpower. Under the umbrella of management, your responsibility is the 5M's. If you, as a senior manager, do not provide these, then it is you that's at fault, not your people!'

I go on to break this down to Mark in more detail.

Means. Methods. Material, Machine and Manpower.

Means:

You must provide all the necessary tooling required to do the job safely and to a high standard of quality.

Methods:

Method statements are clearly defined standards procedure of working practices.

Material:

The Material is of a high standard and fit for purpose.

Machines:

The Machinery is regularly maintained and measured in OEE Overall Equipment Effectiveness.

Manpower:

Everyone has been trained on how to use the equipment they are expected to use to perform their work to a standard that is safe and competent.

So, to summarize: Work within the 3 Principles - Non-blaming, speaking with data and measuring trends not results. Then you must have the seven concepts to work within to achieve what you need to baseline against:

Quality

Cost

Delivery

Productivity

All that equals Profitability.

Then by providing the 5 M's to your management team they will achieve better results than you ever expected.

Mark listened intently to this speech.

Just as I finished, he indicated and pulled up into a car parking space, turning to look at me. 'Well, I certainly hope so, Frank. We're here so let's keep our fingers crossed for some more positivity.'

We entered a very modern building. This was the customer's European headquarters and it had all the trappings of one. Plush sofas in the reception area and, I noted, good photo prints on the wall of their product in application. Always good to see where your product ends up. Surprisingly, not a lot of the workforce know that. Worth doing!

We were inducted via a Health and Safety form and asked to wait to be seen. Jean Luc was the MD, Mark explained and an immovable force.

'Good guy until you piss him off and we have pissed him off, big time.' I could see Mark was a little nervous as was I. Always daunting when you have to go to a valued customer and ask for forgiveness.

'The buyer, Nigel Taylor, he's ok; I get on with him,' Mark continued, 'he's our support here.'

A well-dressed lady came into reception and smiled straight away at Mark, clearly, she knew him.

'Jenny,' Marked beamed.

'Hello Mark, how are you?'

'I'm good thanks, this is our new GM - Frank Walsh.'

Jenny smiled and offered her hand which I shook.

'Nice to meet you Jenny,' I said.

'Likewise,' she turned to Mark, 'follow me they're all waiting for you.'

As we walked Mark and Jenny exchanged pleasantries. I dutifully followed and we entered the Board Room.

Jean Luc was small in stature but certainly had a presence about him and he definitely seemed pissed off judging by the look on his face. Mark made the introductions.

We all sat down and Nigel Taylor began to speak.

'Frank, welcome,' I nodded in response. Jean Luc was staring dispassionately directly at me. I felt a little uneasy.

'It might be good if we gave you some background and a bit of history,' Nigel said.

'I would appreciate that. Thank you.' A PowerPoint presentation beamed up from the table. I automatically looked immediately at the bottom left-hand corner.

This is where you see how many slides are going to be presented and indicates how long the meeting is going to last. Fortunately, it read one of four. The times my heart sinks when it reads one of a hundred plus. You know you're in for a long haul when they start with "I remember when this was all fields!"

'Well, we are a £2 billion global group with markets everywhere. The European division accounts for about 40% of the turnover of which you are one of our top ten strategic suppliers.' I nodded.

'In May last year the problems started.'

Nigel, clearly the consummate professional, hit a button on his laptop and the large display screen on the wall powered into life. On the screen appeared a line graph covering the time period April-April. It wasn't pretty!

'As you can see, this graph represents the On-Time Delivery in Full performance from your site to us here.'

He didn't need to say anything more. A picture paints a thousand words. All of us stared at the screen. I thought the target line of 98.5% was not unreasonable; however, the actual line had plummeted from 68% down to 23%!

'I see,' attempting to placate what was obviously a frustrated team of people. I was speechless for once.

'No, I don't think you do, Mr Walsh!' interrupted Jean Luc with a stern look. I braced myself for incoming as it was clear there was a lot of vented frustration which needed to be released.

'If it wasn't for Nigel here, we would have moved away from this appalling level of service months ago.' I looked at Nigel and nodded an appreciation. Jean Luc continued, 'we are now nearing the end of our surplus stock and if this continues at the current rate, we will have let down our end customer.'

I nodded. No point defending the indefensible.

'I appreciate you have only been here a short time and the fact that you arranged to come and visit your largest customer very quickly is a credit to you.' I acknowledged the sentiments. It was clearly a preamble to a 'BUT.'

'But!' here it comes, I thought. 'It's simply not good enough! You know we have issued a termination letter to your group?'

'Yes, I am aware of that and it's disappointing.'

'We have to go and source another supplier and there are extra costs, or make the components ourselves. We are an Original Equipment Manufacturer (OEM) not a component manufacturer.'

'Yes, I understand.' There was, and is, no point trying to make excuses. This pours oil on the flame. If you take away the oxygen the flame will eventually die by itself.

'Is the ERP system working now?' Jean Luc enquired.

'It is fit for our purpose.' Jean Luc looked bemused so I continued, 'What I mean by that is we were asking the system to perform things we really did not need it to do. We were up to release 3.6. and the team wanted to go to 4.3. All this means is that a lot of people were requesting the system to perform reports and processes not really required for the product. We've stopped all the unnecessary work and releases, allowed the critical ones through which had been sitting in the backlog and have run in a steady state since.'

Jean Luc nodded, 'would like to have, and not must haves?' he enquired.

'Exactly!' I quickly identified that he had some experience of this and I continued, 'Jean-Luc, I would like to make a proposal to you and Nigel.' Clearly recognizing Nigel as a senior manager within the organization would only help things moving forward.

'Please go ahead,' Jean-Luc gestured.

'For the poor level of service, we have provided you I would like to reduce your purchase price to us by 5% effective immediately.' Both were stunned by this; 'and also, effective immediately we are introducing RRS on your product lines.' I continued.

'RRS?' Jean Luc enquired.

'Runners Repeaters and Strangers; RRS.' I continued. 'A runner is a component with high volumes and high frequency and a repeater is a lower volume of product with less frequency. Your FR3103 component would be a runner because it numbers 100,000 every week, your FS457 would be a repeater as it is 50,000 every three weeks. These are the patterns of ordering we have determined from the advance forecast you have given us on a rolling

twelve month. Clearly Strangers are one off, special, etc."
I paused; I now had Jean Luc's attention.

'Forecasting is notoriously inaccurate as we know.
What we can be sure of are the last twelve months sales by
SKU (Stock Keeping Unit) and by volume. We can know
this because we have invoiced you for it. So, we made it
and you've consumed it.' They all nodded in agreement.

'We have analysed*the last twelve-month rolling SKUs
for you. It was determined that 28% of your product
represents 82% of your total order book.' Even Nigel
was surprised at this figure. 'So, using known data and
applying the Pareto rule of 80/20 we have now categorised
all your SKUs into Runners and Repeaters.' I paused.

'So how does this help delivery then Frank? 'Asked
Nigel.

'We will move away from the traditional way of
manufacturing your products which is a push system,
and move to a pull system,' I paused. 'A pull system is
an information system for controlling and improving the
flow of materials and information. It is then possible to
allocate resources based on actual consumption not on
forecast demand.'

'The most significant source of waste is overproduction
which means producing more, sooner or faster than is
required by the next process.'

'Moving from Push to Pull production has the
single greatest impact on improving material flow and

eliminating waste. It also has the effect of significantly improving OTIF. (On Time in Full) delivery, a step change if you will. The inherent problem associated with the push system is production based on anticipated needs.' I reeled them off and the audience was silent but listening intently so I continued;

'We propose to move from Forecast driven demand to Date Driven scheduling. It is possible to fix repeat scheduling on key machines to ensure any product shipped is automatically replenished. Dedicated machines dedicated to your product. We are moving away from the traditional view that infinite capacity is assumed, where no account is made for workload levels or the number of available people on machine or cell. Now it is correct capacity planned with 85% efficiency. Using the pull system means that we can reduce costs and drive performance.

'Carry on,' said John-Luc as I paused for breath and allowed the room to process.

'With the traditional push model, we can see that any issue in the planning and production process means that lead times expand and maintaining flow is costly. Inventory increases. The wrong inventory increases and the correct stock is not being produced in the qualities required. The definition of the pull system is produce only what is ordered, when it is ordered and, in the quantities, required. The upstream process produces only enough units to replace those that have been withdrawn by the downstream process.'

'Makes sense,' Nigel commented.

'Yes, it does. It's like going to a fast-food outlet. They only produce what they sell using a pull system which is based on demand. Look at the big M. They operate the perfect example of a Kanban system and this means that they ensure a reduction in excess inventory and product obsolescence.

Since component parts are not delivered until just before they are needed, there is a reduced need for storage space. Should a product or component design be upgraded, that upgrade can be included in the final product ASAP. There is no inventory of products or components that become obsolete.'

'Well, that's interesting as we have quite a bit of obsolescent stock here, also,' Nigel commented. The room tension lessened and I could see I was making sense to them so I continued.

'Yes, the Kanban system reduces waste and scrap as products and components are only manufactured when they are needed. This eliminates overproduction. Raw materials are not delivered until they are needed reducing waste and cutting storage costs. It is all Just In Time (JIT).

The other benefits it provides is flexibility in production. If there is a sudden drop in demand for a product Kanban ensures you are not stuck with excess inventory. This gives you the flexibility to rapidly respond to a changing demand. At the same time, it actually increases Outputs as the flow of Kanban (cards, bins, pallets, etc.) will stop if there is a production problem. Stopping production worries Operations, but actually they need to realise that production doesn't automatically increase efficiency. By stopping production and problem solving there and then makes problems visible quickly, allowing them to be corrected ASAP.

Kanban reduces wait times by making supplies more accessible and breaking down administrative barriers. This results in an increase in production using the same resources.' I was now on the soap box again; I paused; the room was thoughtful.

'It's easy to make things difficult but difficult to make things easy,' I concluded, 'but I need your help, Jean-Luc.' He looked up; I always try and make the opponent part of the solution to a problem.

'But how can I help?' he asked. I leaned forward.

'If you would allow two of your engineers or one engineer and one operator to come to our plant as our guests.'

He nodded but looked worried.

'We will pay for all the expenses incurred.'

Jean Luc was even more interested.

'Why do you need my staff?'

'I propose they form part of our Kaizen Team at our facility to put into place the pull systems I just described. They will be an integral part of the redesigning to cost element of the Kaizen. We will also take out extra costs and I ask we split the difference in the sales unit cost

50/50 after you've taken the 5% discount I've already offered.'

I paused to evaluate their reaction. Nigel clearly liked it because it meant he didn't have to try and resource another supplier which doubtless would have to be one of the emerging countries: China, India, Brazil or another South American country less friendly to the West. The pain of ramping up a new supplier with the inevitable rejects and delays would be an extra disruption factor.

'Tell me what this Kaizen event consists of?' asked Jean-Luc. I could see Mark in my peripheral vision rolling his eyes as if to say 'here we go again!' In fact, I could hear his eyes rolling!

I started to explain the theory of Kaizen and what it meant to the business.

I concluded and the room became silent. Both Jean Luc and Nigel were nodding in agreement.

'Well Frank, that sounds impressive' declared Jean Luc. 'We will send you two of our engineers to support this bold programme.'

'Thank you so much.'

We adjourned and left the room shaking hands; the atmosphere was a little more cordial.

We got in the car and both sat in silence. Mark broke the spell.

'Well,' he said, 'Frank you did it, we've got a stay of execution.'

'Yes,' I replied thoughtfully as Mark started the car.

'Now all you've got to do is deliver it.'

'We all have to deliver it Mark - not me, but us.'

Mark looked me in the eye like a rabbit caught in headlights, then he drove off at speed.

CHAPTER 14

How Many Squares?

We returned to the Plant. I went straight to see Scott to see how he was performing against the red-hot list issued by Sales that week; also I took a look at the DMS board. In a snapshot I could see how the plant was performing and any issues which needed to be addressed as a matter of priority. Scott saw me and shot over.

'Hi Scott, how are you doing?'

'I'm OK.' That was pleasing to hear.

'I guess you want to see the updates?'

'Of course! This time every day.' Scott smiled.

It's very important and it doesn't matter how onerous or tiresome it gets, you have to be totally consistent in your approach.

Remember…. no meeting before 2pm.

Remember… it's up to you to walk around. After all, patients in hospital don't go and see the doctor, the consultant goes to them to give them his prognosis and more importantly the cure.

'ATS this morning is 83%,' Scott beamed.

'Fantastic!' I declared. Another boost to his battered ego. 'Any problems?' I asked.

'No, just that prat. Julian, trying to sneak in more of his own orders. Sod everyone else!' He certainly wasn't a team player, this Julian.

'You managed to fob him off?'

'Oh yes!' Scott grinned. "Let's say he's been re-calibrated.' Scott grinned like a Cheshire cat.

'If Adherence to Schedule is 83% then the OTIF in the next 24 hours will be high again.

'Well done!' I nodded my appreciation and left him on the shop floor where he belonged.

I strode back to my office feeling in control; however, this was short lived. Stuart, the Financial Controller, was standing in my doorway. He must have spotted Mark and assumed I was in.

'Hi Stuart,' I gestured, 'how are you?'

'You won't believe what they want me to do now!' he cried.

I stopped; common courtesy and politeness are free and they set the tone of any meeting.

'Hello Frank, how are you? Did the meeting at our top customer go well?' I spoke.

Stuart grimaced, 'sorry Frank.' I walked past him into my office. 'It's just that Head Office is going over the top with this visit from the States next week.'

'How come?' I asked.

'They asked me to produce all these slides,' Stuart gave me a hard copy of the email he had been sent by Central Finance. I started to read it.

'Email them back and acknowledge that you have received it but that you do not have the time to produce this as you are producing the recovery plan presentation for me.'

Stuart went quiet; I looked up; 'What's the matter?'

'Could you send it?' he asked. I immediately sat down at my desk and opened all my draws one by one, slamming them shut as I did so. I then went to the waste bin and started rummaging through it, much to Stuart's bemusement.

'What you looking for?' he asked.

'Your balls!' I replied.

Stuart sent the email.

Once the email had been sent, I knew it would be only a matter of time before Central Finance would call. The phone duly rang.

'Hi Frank, its Dave Hurst from Central Finance.'

'Afternoon Dave.'

'Frank, I have just had an email from Stuart and he is refusing to help. It's just that we need to put this slide pack together for the meeting on Monday with the Americans; you know how important it is.'

'Firstly, Stuart is not refusing to help you; he is working for me. I am aware that they're coming all the way over here to learn what our recovery plan is going to be.'

'Precisely! So, we need to put this pack together pronto. Didier wants to see it before it goes and we are tight for time!'

'Who's stopping you putting your pack together?' I asked.

'Well, Stuart is telling me you instructed him to work on the recovery plan.'

'That's correct; after all that's why they're coming over, right?'

'Yes, but Roger Rewinkle wants this pack put together.' A grown-up.

'I'm sure he does but let me put one thing straight here; until we, the team who will deliver the recovery plan, agree on how we are going to do it, there is no plan. I do not want more versions of the truth no matter who requested it.' I never understand why people throw a name or position in your face when they are not getting their way, as if that is supposed to scare you.

'Frank why are you being difficult?' Dave asked, exasperated.

'Dave, I'm not being difficult! You have a whole team of financial controllers down there; I've only got Stuart. If you want to put an 85-slide pack together to just go over what happened in the previous twelve months then by all means do it. As if Roger doesn't know all that anyway. I want to put together the recovery plan for this financial year.' There was silence at the other end.

'Well, I'm going to have to mention this to Didier.' Another name! Another threat!

'You do what you have to do and I shall do what I have to do, but remember Dave, you never drive forward looking in the rear-view mirror. Now, if you don't mind, I have work to do.' I put the phone down.

When I'd returned from my Gemba walk I could see there were several missed calls from Andrew. This was also expected and I called back.

'Afternoon Andrew, how can I help?' I said in a chipper voice.

'Well,' came the reply. 'Stop pissing off the finance team would be a start.'

'Andrew, I told you that we are in lockdown. The only support I wanted from you and the executive team was to be left alone, and for you to field off the unnecessary time-wasting meetings and reports. This company is going to the wall; it's not self-sufficient yet and you are all treating it as business as usual; is it any wonder you got yourselves in this mess?'

There was a silence at the end of the phone so I continued, 'if you cannot help then don't hinder.'

'This is the governance they expect Frank,' Andrew declared. I sighed, sat down, and calmly began to talk to Andrew.

'Yes, and how's that worked out for you?' I asked. Silence at the end of the phone and a standoff I knew

I really should defuse. I took a deep breath. 'Andrew let me tell you a story if I may. It's the true story of Bernie Madoff, a New York trader in the stock exchange who created a multibillion empire from a scheme they call Ponzi. It took willing people's money on the promise of a great return and gave dividends way above the normal market rate. This then inspired more investors and all along it was nothing but a pyramid game. Eventually after 15 years it was discovered to be a scam when people wanted their money back after the 2008 crash. There was no money left! Fifty billion pounds squandered on personal gain for the Madoffs. He is currently serving 150 years in prison.

'Yes, yes!' Andrew said impatiently. 'What's this got to do with governance?'

'So, I started to think why was the scheme not discovered earlier? The Financial Regulation Authority is probably one of the most stringent in the world. Auditors auditing auditors, governing bodies constantly reviewing; so, the governance of an organization is crucial to address fraud and performance related bonuses. So, what is your organization governance like?'

I pause, resisting the urge to use the word "terrible" just yet.

'It's well…' Andrew spluttered, 'it's how it's always been!'

'Andrew, you have weekly, monthly, quarterly, half yearly and annual reviews and always there is a surprise for everyone. When you did forecast a positive EBITA number for the first quarter of your fiscal you soon realised that only two months in you would post a loss of over half a million!'

There was silence at the end of the phone.

'My question is, if the governance is so crucial to the organization why has it been so wrong? Governance works but only if it's effective. The reason why Madoff wasn't discovered earlier was because of the arrogance and egos of the governing powers. Bureaucracy and political infighting create an unhealthy environment in which to govern. What's this organization's governance like? Changing timelines? Forecasts? Ever moving targets? All set by centralized accountants without an exposure to the actual markets and businesses. Correct me if I'm wrong but both the CEO and the CFO were fired by the States for this level of incompetence?'

'True.' Andrew admitted.

'And we still have the financial governance with the same people? If you always do what you've always done you will always get what you've always had. I'm telling you now, Andrew, it won't be long before there's another scandal where your governance will fail, and you will be left with a feeling that somebody made off with your business.'

'I see what you did there; Madoff, made off, funny!' Andrew settled down, deflated.

'Andrew we simply do not have enough precious time left before the Monday meeting. I want to spend what time we do have on the recovery plan to overcome the problem, not on producing eighty slides addressing what happened last year.'

'I know, I know; my job is to keep you away from all this. You carry on. Didier and I will sort it.'

'Thanks Andrew and thanks for the support.' Quite frankly, I didn't actually feel that he had given me the support I would have expected. His behaviour was not what I would expect from a COO.

'By the way, pretty ballsy move there about not having to do the Sunday call.' Andrew's voice softened, 'that's the "fist in the air moment for your team". I guess they found a leader?'

I smiled, 'It's only because you put me there,' I said, wondering why he didn't intervene himself to support his people.

'Anyway, this had better be good on Monday Frank.' Andrew changed his tone, back to business in his usual style.

I smiled; I knew exactly what the Americans wanted. A clear plan for recovery with the foundation stones laid for the next fiscal year to bring it back to business as usual. Then they could have all their meetings and PowerPoint presentations to their hearts content because I wouldn't be there.

I called the team for a meeting. They arrived on time in the boardroom (2pm). I was already there. I set the stage and revealed a standard square picture divided into 16 squares four by four.

'Right team, you've got one minute. Look at this square, very simple very basic. I want you each in silence, you too Scott,' I looked at Scott and he smiled, 'to write down the number of squares you see. No conferring just looks for one minute.' I timed it on my mobile.

How Many Squares Do You See?

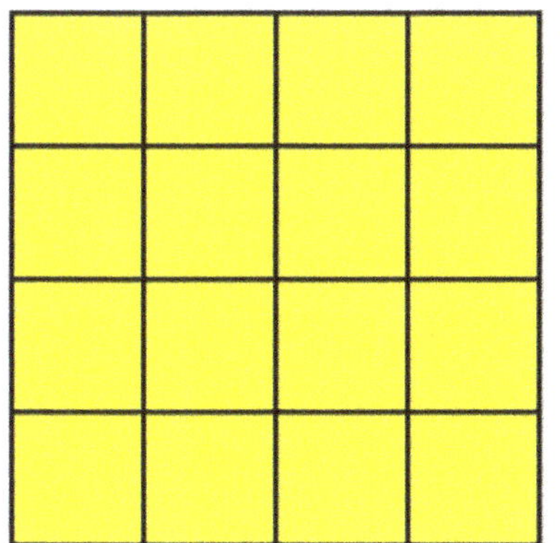

One minute passed.

'Scott?'

'22' he replied.

'Salma? '

'19' she replied.

'Sarah?'

'17'

'Mark?'

'25'

'Daniel?'

'22'

'Graham?'

'19'

'Paula?'

'21'

'Heather?'

'23'

'Stuart?'

'26'

'Jason?'

'17'

I wrote down all the different answers on the board.

'So, team what can we deduce from this?' I looked around the room and people shuffled in their seats.

'People see things differently?' piped up Paula.

'Precisely! We're all looking at the same thing within the same time constraints in exactly the same environment and yet we came up with several different answers.' They nodded in agreement.

'So, if we are going to come up with a recovery plan which, let's face it, is going to be a lot more complex, we have got to be all seeing the same thing.'

'By the way there are 30 squares.' I started to draw where they were on the four-by-four diagram and it was met with oohs! and arrs.

How many squares?

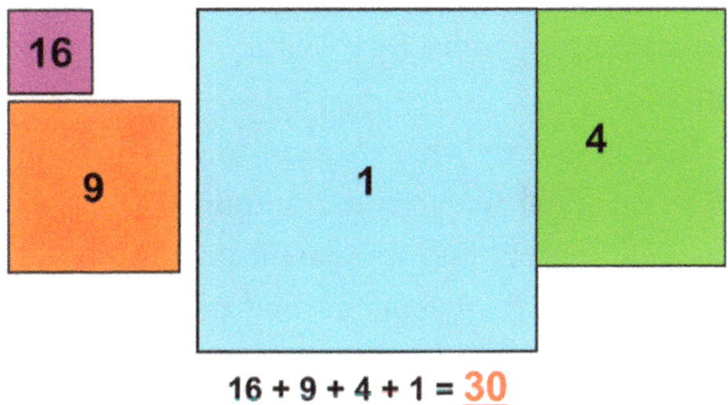

'Right team, we have the visit here on Monday of the American owners. They want to see how we are getting on, and more importantly, how they can help.' I looked around the room.

'Help?' Scott chuckled sarcastically.

'That's right. They're here to help so let's take advantage of the fact that; a. we are a relatively new team and; b. the problem wasn't our fault. We've identified headcount savings generating a 70/30 split from direct hands to in-directs. Paula, please prepare and present your slide. We haven't named names just the departments in which they work. This summarises the total headcount reduction and more importantly when they are going to be phased out?'

'Yes, will do,' said Paula.

'Waste is a big factor. We need machinery that can re-inject back into the process the waste caused by start-ups, trim, etc. Graham, I need an estimate of costs for reinjection machines so we can reduce waste and also reduce procuring unnecessary virgin material, if we decide to do it.'

'I know exactly what we need,' declared Graham.

'Scott, good work on the output. Let's use our unit of measure output and compare it to last month and the month before. Remember second principle of Kaizen?' I waited. Daniel was first in.

'Measure trends not results.'

'Exactly!'

'Swot!' joked Mark to Daniel.

'Teacher's pet!' added Scott, but Daniel took it in good humour. It is important to keep energy high in this kind of event.

'Good! Costs please, Stuart, I need you to compile this in a standard Waterfall. Start with the £1.9m deficit and with all the add-ons and takeaways we should end up with by the end of the fiscal year at a minus £600k position. One slide, not 85.'

'Thank God!' exclaimed Stuart.

'Sarah,' Sarah perked up.

'I need the cost of non-quality items, the cost of rejects and that of returns from our customer. Break it all down into those three characters.' She nodded.

'Jason, Health & Safety; we have a good record here so let's blow our trumpet on it.'

'Salma, Customer Care please - on one slide. Show how we are performing against OTIF R and OTIF P. In the last three weeks we have seen a significant step change in performance so let's get it out there.'

'Will do, some good news to show for a change.'

'Mark, please highlight the pipeline of additional sales and then raise the visit we made to our number one customer this week. I will then talk through the initiatives we discussed.'

I paused; they were all scribbling down notes.

'We will each present our own slides. This is not my show, this is our show.' They all nodded in agreement except Graham. I could see it frightened the living daylights out of him. We would work on that later, I noted.

It's important that the host team can actively demonstrate to the owners what they have input into the recovery plan and their part in it. After all, they were all going to have to sustain it after I was long gone.

'Right, any questions? Are we all seeing 30 squares?' They all laughed as they jumped out of their chairs ready to get their slides prepared. 'Remember team, send all the slides and no more than four each to Stuart to compile.' 'Stuart, I want 32 slides maximum.'

'Then back here to discuss support and help. Remember clear your diaries; this is the most important item on your to-do list. We all clear, team?'

They beamed with confidence and left the boardroom. I noted the time - all this in less than an hour.

CHAPTER 15

Preparation for the New Ways

The weekend went by without incident. I arrived early on the Monday, not to polish the gravel because the grownups were coming, but I wanted to make sure everything was going according to plan. Failure to prepare means you're prepared to fail. I was not going to fail on these people's livelihoods.

Scott was already doing the rounds. I spotted him going from daily system boards throughout the plant. He'd got the routine spot on and wasn't ever going to revert back to the hour and a half meeting. I went into Stuart's office to make sure he wasn't being roped back into the "faceless finance fraternity" as I respectfully called it. He wasn't in!

I went to my office and turned on my email, then went to get a coffee while it was replicating. Daniel was already at the machine. and he beamed a big smile.

'Can I get you a coffee boss?'

'Sure, thanks,' I said. Daniel had really rebuilt his confidence and I could see he was engaging with all his managers and peers alike.

'So, Daniel how many things are you involved in now?'

Daniel smiled, 'just four things,' he said.

I smiled back. One of the lessons I teach all my managers is that with all the projects and initiatives going on, if you insist on getting involved in too many you will fail in all of them. Just do four things, finish those four, then build on them with another four. That way you will actually achieve something. It then becomes self-perpetuating and confidence starts to grow as you see results coming in. It's great to see managers and people grow before your very eyes. Daniel was a particularly good pupil.

Display your four things on a white board in your office. It serves as a reminder when you start to deviate from them and it's a good focal point.

Operational Roadmap 2018

Name	Project 1	Project 2	Project 3	Project 4
Nicola	Minimum on hand	Place order for temporary storage	Implement MES	Site 5s
Dave	Rollout of DMS in production	SMED / Changeover reduction	Material Waste Reduction	5s
Ben	Preventative Maint	SMED / Changeover	Site 5s	Compressor Room and Workshop
Helen	Minimum on hand	Case management (Epicor)	Rollout of DMS in customer service	Sample room and archive storage
Grant	Rearrange yard (incl tent)	Establish and maintain goods in procedure	Warehouse Optimisation (Epicor)	Standard Operations
Jim	Case Management	Standard Operations	QC Capacity	Lineside QC
Frank				

Please Complete then Replicate Tier Down

'So, Daniel, have you ever been exposed to a kaizen event?' I asked knowing what would be an enthusiastic response from him; he had an insatiable appetite to learn. I cannot teach this genuine work ethic or dedication, but what I can teach is the methodologies you need to adopt to be successful.

'I've been doing my homework but I haven't actually done one before.'

'Well, there's one happening at the end of the month and I want you to lead one of the three teams.'

'Really? That would be great! Are you sure?' Daniel questioned; always lacking in self-belief.

'Yes, most definitely!' We carried our coffees towards my office. 'Let me show you what I mean by the kaizen event.' As we walked to my office I started to tell him about Lean and Six Sigma.

"So, what's the difference between Lean and Six Sigma?" Asked Daniel.

"Well Six Sigma is a methodology to measure variability in a process. Then it seeks to find out what the variabilities are; this can be a deep dive analysis and can take some time to be proven. Lean, addresses the fundamental flow of a process from bottom up, eliminating waste of all kinds. Also Lean is typical, logical and easy to understand, whereas Sigma is a little more complex. Try implementing sigma to the shop floor operators - it's all Greek to them!' I declared, a favourite saying of mine. Daniel laughed and I continued to explain.

'Seriously, there's a place for both; it's just that in this case we need the grass roots logical approach to eliminate waste. Get quick wins which builds confidence in people. Sigma comes later when we clear the decks and need to home in on the variability of each process.'

Daniel nodded in agreement.

I started to write on the board and continued;

'Kaizen blitz is a week-long focus group identifying a single problem and coming up with a new way of working to overcome the problem. We do this by using Kaizen methodologies. We know the principles and the concepts so now I want to show you some of the tools we will use.'

'The cornerstone of any improvement is 5S. Are you familiar with 5S Daniel?'

'Never done one but it's housekeeping, right?'

'Not really. It's a series of steps to ensure the place of work we are dealing with provides us with the environment where any abnormality jumps right out at us. A place for everything and everything in its place.'

'So, if I look across the factory floor, I should be able to see an empty plastic cup or a crisp packet from any view point. Do we have that currently?'

'No!' Daniel said definitely.

I continued, 'if a device would save just 10 per cent in time or increase results by 10 per cent, then its absence will always be a 10 per cent Tax,' I declared. 'Henry Ford said that!'

'Save ten steps a day for each of your employees and you will have saved kilometres of wasted motion and misspent energy.' Daniel nodded.

'Did he say that? I thought 5S was born in Japan?'

'No, in Michigan with Henry Ford – not in Japan. It began with the need to reduce defects and problems when assembling interchangeable parts in automobiles. Two of Henry Ford's mantras were:

"We cannot afford to have dirt around— it is too expensive,"

and

"Your wastebasket is your friend."

'The culture of America at the time included the unquestioned discipline that stemmed from "the need to keep your rifle just so." In the late 1800's and early 1900's rifles could be just as unreliable as the powder used to fire them. Ford utilized this militia thinking as he implemented Standard Work around how you kept your place of work clean, because dirt and early interchangeable parts did not mix. Same with guns, if you did not take care of your rifle it would not take care of you.

Daniel nodded his understanding.

'This is a history lesson Daniel; it started with '3S' and that stood for Smoke, Soot, and Smudge. 5S as we know it did not come along until the 1950's. I started to explain the concept to him:

To Henry Ford CANDO was "Workplace Organization." It was renamed by the Japanese in the '50s into five Japanese words that were easier for their employees to remember. North Americans knowing nothing about

CANDO spotted 5S in Japan and brought it back to North America, and then agonized over what five English words would equate to the actions associated with 5S.

Here are the 5 practices that so many attribute to coming from a land far away when they really came from Michigan.

5S is one of the foundation stones to build upon. It is a beginning of a culture and I have dedicated a lot of time to it as it is truly the catalyst for real change; without it you will always fail. Humans are visual beings who have learned 83% of what they know through their eyes. After all isn't that how we all learn? From seeing and doing?

For the academics the real 5S are as follows: Sort, Set in Order, Shine, Standardize, and Sustain.

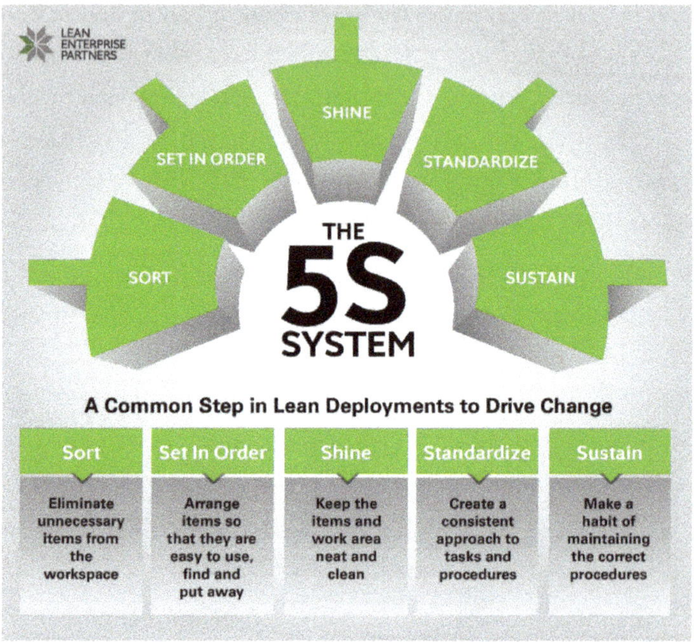

The biggest challenge in implementing 5S is making it sustainable, a habit and a mindset that forms part of the real work.

We think we know it backwards but, in my experience, the actual way of 5S is as follows:

1st S – Start: 2nd S– Slip: 3rd S-Slide: 4th S – Stop: 5th S – Start Again

The 6th S is of course Safety. If one thing comes out of 5S that is worth more than any productivity figures it's Safety. One third of all accidents reported are down to poor housekeeping. You can get incredible improvements of safely with good 5S. I have seen achievements of 67% improvement on Lost Time Accidents (LTA) and 27% improvement on reported accidents.

Why is it so hard? We know the theory but what is it about sustaining 5S? Why is it so difficult?

The practical definition of Leadership is 'the ability to gather followers.' Such a management style includes 'lead by example' in the behavior of its leaders. An excellent earlier example of an insightful leader who would not allow 5S to proceed until all managers had '5Sd' the areas where they lived… their offices, is an excellent one. The managers will have more empathy with their employees by doing this, and in the end will be more effective leaders.

I remember a time when my Finance Director declared "I want to 5S my office!" so I volunteered to go to his office at 6pm that day and 5S it with him.

What I found was a total mess as well as a breeding ground for trip hazards! In an office.

When we had finished three hours later the place looked different but it was too traumatic for the FD who had nearly burst into tears when I removed all his filing cabinets. He declared that he needed the filing cabinets.

'OK then. How many pieces of paper does one draw hold?' I asked him.

Thousands!' he declared.

'Three thousand pieces of paper in one draw. You're the finance guy so that's 12,000 in one four drawer cabinet. How many filing cabinets do you have?' We counted – there were 8, therefore ninety-six thousand pieces of paper stored. He nodded in agreement until I asked him when was the last time, he ever went to a filing cabinet and took something out.

5S in the Office environment is the toughest.

This finance director? Well, despite everything he gradually reverted back to his own ways and never once led the rest of the finance office by example and yet he demanded 5S.

From watching behavioural patterns at work around housekeeping there seems to be an unwritten understanding that 'I don't do housekeeping' among many people around 45-60 years of age. (I'm not being ageist here; I'm old enough to remember when grandparents' names were Dick and Fanny!) But it is a culture which stems from a lack of appreciation of what the role of 5S really is, and that's the fault of management. In analysing many 5S collapses it was noticed that a high percentage of older people were the first to drift away from a 5S process that began with such great promise. They went back to doing their thing.

Real life example! How many calendars can you see?

Five. Five calendars and he still didn't know what day it was!

I finished my lesson and turned to look at Daniel. 'When we launch a 5S campaign we always identify a pilot area first. Don't try a blitz on the whole factory, you won't have the resources or the time. So many companies make that error of judgement. This feeds the doubting Thomases and the nay-sayers when things go wrong, so it's very important that we pilot an area and really make it work.'

Daniel nodded, 'Yes, I can see that'.

'So now you see that, back to the Kaizen event, but remember the 5S lesson; it will come in useful very soon as it is something we will be implementing.'

'First thing we do is form a cross functional team: 30% must come from the work area, 30% management, 30% functional support. These can either be suppliers and/or other people within the company's portfolio, like your sister company up the road. That way you do not put too much strain on the local resources.'

Daniel nodded.

'Be careful who you pick; they have got to be of the right mind set in the first Kaizen event. Like with the 5S, it's got to work.'

I wrote 12 people's names on the board, then I split the names into thirds.

'Team 1 which you will be heading up Daniel will be the 5S element of the Kaizen event. Told you the lesson would come in useful.'

Daniel nodded in agreement.

'Team 2 will be the value stream mapping element; identifying value added and non-value-added processes throughout the cycle of the product. I will oversee this group.'

'What else Frank?'

'We then have Team 3. They will be the technical support in identifying cost out of the product itself. Redesign to cost. This is what we promised our customer so I'm going to ask Fabrizio, the R&D Director, to run this element.'

'What about involving Scott in this?' Daniel asked.

'Well to be honest, I know Scott would love to be part of it. However, someone has got to do the day job. No matter how many times we want to do this over the next year, I recommend at least one Kaizen event every month. Around nine in a year. Someone has got to hold the store and Scott has got momentum now; we need him to keep the product moving out the door.'

'Are we going to have to stop the line for this?' Daniel enquired.

'No, we can work around the shift patterns and the people.'

'Sounds like a good plan; when do we start?'

'Right then, glad you asked that! 'No time like the present!' I grinned and rubbed my hands. 'Daniel who should be on the list for your team?'

We worked for forty minutes deciding who was going to be on which team. The two volunteers from our customers were to support Fabricio in the Redesign to Cost group.

Daniel and I concluded the first planning meeting and I walked with him to the Daily Management System stand up with his Customer Services Department. Remember you only use a deputy when you are not on site, not because you're busy. Attendance was mandatory for everyone including myself. We agreed to carry on after lunch with the planning of the Kaizen.

I then went to see Fabrizio. He had been off my radar so far for all the right reasons but it was time to engage with an immovable force. Fabrizio was the Italian born, technical director for the group. He had an exceptional brain and an amazing depth of knowledge of the properties of the product we made. Being Italian, he would enthuse any meeting or idea with his Italian gusto. However, the down side to such a borderline genius was his total inability to organise, and his communication left something to be desired - but what an exceptional mind.

It never fails to shock me, but I always feel flabbergasted when I go to businesses with an excellent engineering pedigree and research and development programmes but terrible man management. Ensuring new products get developed is the future life blood of a business and yet so many R&D departments are run by people who should not be in that position. I am not saying they shouldn't be in senior positions, but I see it frequently: Highly qualified people with excellent degrees in engineering, and what do senior directors in the businesses do to them? They make them managers of large departments with all the HR administration and personnel issues to deal with, areas in which they have limited natural ability such as quarterly appraisals, holiday scheduling and so on.

New Products Introduction and New Designs fall by the way side while they deal with these issues. I have not met one engineering or R&D Manager who made a good departmental manager. I believe it is in their make-up that they struggle with the day-to-day administration as they all try to get things to a perfect state. They are great at what they are trained to do! So, let them get on and do it!

I always thought that the parliamentary process of having private secretaries to do all the necessary administration so the Ministers can get on with the job of creating policies and implementing them worked well. Maybe it's time we looked at moving away from the traditional way of running a department (the most senior people become head) and just give the office admin the support they crave for. You don't hire a brain surgeon and not give him a scalpel?

I entered the R&D department where Fabrizio was at his desk pondering over some drawings.

'Good morning Fabrizio.' I got a warm handshake and an enthusiastic smile.

'Please call me Fab.' His accent was thick and reminded me of summers in Italy. Not the time nor the place to be reminiscing, I reminded myself, and distracted myself by observing the muddle surrounding the mad professor. The office was adorned with samples, paperwork and a lot of mess. I'm sure Fab knew where everything was if he needed to get to it but I just couldn't for the life of me see how anyone could work in such chaos. Each to their own!

'Fab I need your help!' I said. Always be the passive asking for help; it automatically endears you to the other person as all they want to do is to support you. If you go in with an attitude of "I want you to do this" they feel like they're being told to volunteer (rolling tiered) and not asked.

'Sure Mr. Walsh, how can I help you?'

'Well, you know that we're in danger of losing our biggest customer account?'

'Yes, very bad, very sad; we have worked many years with them.'

'Well, I went to see them and they are willing to give us one last chance.' Fabrizio's eyes suddenly widened.

'Really?' He was taken aback.

'Yes,' I said. However we need to demonstrate that we can do it.'

'Yes please! Yes please!' Fabrizio was now getting excited. Difficult to contain.

'They are sending two engineers over to us to help redesign the product to reduce cost.'

'Who they sending?' he asked.

'Jonty Morgan and Pierre Beeson.' Fabrizio clapped his hands loudly.

'My friends! Love them both! They are good engineers. I work with them many, many times.' I was pleased to hear this as three mad professors in one space for a whole week could cause problems if they didn't get on.

'Great! I'll send out the invites to you. We need to bring this one home Fabrizio; we have a lot of livelihoods depending on us.'

'You can depend on me, Mr. Walsh, for sure.' I got up, smiled and walked away. Despite the fact he was as mad as a box of frogs he was genuinely skilful and dedicated. We would definitely need him for this one. He was a rabbit, which was great, but I just needed to harness that energy.

Vinnie Paul was a large man with a big smile and heart. He was Fabrizio's right-hand man and the one responsible for the department actually running projects on time and within budget.

'How's it going chief?' he beamed.

'Very well Vinnie. How are you?'

'I'm good boss; all is well.'

'I've got the mad professor on a week-long project coming up soon, in the next couple of weeks actually, and I need you to hold the fort for a while?'

'Sure, no problem, always do,' he smiled. It's a good thing we have Vinnie Pauls in the organization. Where would we be without them?

Daniel returned to my office after lunch and we continued with the Kaizen preparations. Like any event it required meticulous planning and some foresight to start ordering things we'd need. Paint for the floor, new signage for the areas, all the practical items required for real change.

After we had made the shopping list of all we thought we would need for a successful Kaizen event, I went about looking at the presentation Stuart had put together for the grown-ups' meeting on Monday. Remember failure to prepare means you're prepared to fail. I knew how important this meeting would be to re-instil confidence in the shareholders, as well as in the team. Relief flooded through me as I read through the deck he had prepared.

'Excellent pack Stuart! Well done!' Stuart smiled in response to the praise. 'Tells the story of the past and, more importantly, the future.'

'Yes, it does. I'm happy with the sequence, are you?'

'Fine! It reads well.'

'I've been asked to send it to Didier first, if that's all right?'

'Sure, send it to whoever you wish but no amendments or changes are to be made. OK?'

'I will tell them.'

The stage was set for the very important meeting on Monday. I left the office on time and drove away for a nice relaxing weekend. My phone was turned off.

CHAPTER 16

The Grown Ups

The air was charged with anxiety on that Monday morning. The visitors from the United States were in transit and due to arrive in the plant at around 1 o'clock. I made sure everything was as normal as possible. We did all the Daily Management Systems meetings as usual.

Helen was busying herself organizing the boardroom and lunch for the six visitors. I was pleased to note the new visitor board in reception which had been put in place since my first recommendation.

I went through the presentation once more and mentally rehearsed what I would say. I'm sure some challenging questions were going to be put to me and the team. We'd had a very good month end the previous month so we were on a high. A dangerous place to be when improving. It wasn't time to breathe just yet. We hadn't turned the corner but the daily disciplines and the time saved from unnecessary meetings and conference calls allowed us to really focus on the important issues and deal with them then and there. What I call JFDI. Just flipping, doing it or words to that effect.

On time delivery was rising, particularly the OTIF P. With the fixed rolling five-day plan combined with the red-hot lists from sales performance we were on the up and, more importantly, staying up and consistent. There were lots of things to show and tell the visitors about and I was quietly confident we would get an easy ride. Interestingly, Andrew wasn't going to be at this initial meeting as he had other priorities. I thought that was very strange.

The limo drew up in the visitor's car park (now there were plenty of empty spaces to choose from!) I heard the clunk of car doors and they walked to reception where I was waiting to greet them all.

'Welcome,' I said, with an outstretched hand. I smiled and a tall well-built man with floppy sand-coloured hair smiled back and shook my hand warmly.

In a deep southern-American accent he said, 'Roger Rewinkle, pleased to meet you.' I still had a good feeling.

'Mark Lee,' another tall American; 'Senior Vice President, Global Operations,' he too shook my hand warmly. 'I've heard a lot about you, Frank.'

'Not bad I hope.'

'On the contrary,' Mark beamed.

'Gary Parker,' a smaller American this time, but still taller than me. 'Global Group Finance Operations Director.'

I nodded in acknowledgement.

'Bob Border, Group IT Director.' I had spoken to Bob several times on the phone about the ERP implementation and the stopping of further iterations. He'd liked my mobile phone analogy.

'Hank Lewinski, Senior Vice President of Technical Services.'

'Hank.' Finally, we came to the last guest.

'Surinder Ranjit, Financial Director for the Group.' I shook his hand.

'Gentlemen, may I ask that you watch the health and safety video please as part of your induction.' I gestured towards the television screen mounted on the wall.

They all obliged. We sat quietly in the boardroom and while the video ran, I asked Helen if she would organize the site senior management team to join us.

Before long the team joined us all in the boardroom with perfect timing as the video finished. I was impressed with Roger as he stood up and personally greeted each of my team in turn. This put them a little more at ease. I could detect their nervousness.

We all sat down and I opened the meeting.

'Welcome all of you. I think it would be worthwhile for Roger if we all introduce ourselves in turn.'

'Great idea Frank let's do it.' Roger beamed as I turned to my team.

'OK team, would you give you name, your position and the length of time you have been here.'

Sarah started. 'Hi, I'm Sarah Collinsworth; I'm the Quality Manager and I have been here for 8 months.'

'Graham Paul; Engineering Manager, 22 years.'

'Daniel Lockett; Supply Chain Manager and I've been here 18 months.'

'Paula Bartram; HR manager, just 4 months for me.'

'Stuart Carr; I am the Financial Controller and I've been here 6 months.'

'Mark Winter; Sales Director, 20 months.'

'Scott Mullen; Production Manager, been here 18 months.'

All were acknowledged.

'Our turn, suggested Roger so we went around the other side of the table so that everyone knew who they were talking with. Always a good idea and a way of reducing the tension.

I started the presentation with the first slide which showed the chaos we were in, mainly due to the implementation of the new ERP system and the haphazard approach to updates. I emphasized this was the catalyst that identified the hidden issues the business was dealing with. We went through the financials and ended with the slide they were all here for. The recovery plans.

When I finished Surinder asked the 64-million-dollar question.

'When, in the next fiscal, do you think we will be making the profit we would expect to see?'

'First quarter period of next fiscal we will see an EBITDA in double digits.' I was direct and to the point as this is the way Americans like it. No waffle and no bullshit but I was also being mindful not to give an exact number. There's always someone who writes it down and then comes back to you at a later date to bite you on the arse with it.

Roger spoke next. 'How confident are you, Frank, in these predictions here?'

'Fairly confident Roger; I've got a good team around me.' Roger nodded his acceptance.

Mark Lee spoke; his voice was loud. 'That's a hell of a lot to do in a short period of time.'

'Yes Mark. It is.'

'What can we do to help?' Mark asked.

'We need investment in some pieces of kit.'

Hank quizzed, 'What type of kit?'

Surinder asked, 'And how much?'

Graham stepped in and did a really good job of convincing Hank and Roger of the need for the new kit. This was Graham at his best. No slides to present, just hard facts and passion in his belief. He had been at the company all his working life and what he didn't know in terms of the equipment wasn't worth knowing. When Graham finished his pitch, Stuart announced '£750k.'

Roger sat thoughtfully, 'OK, go ahead. Raise the capexs over for signature.'

'Thank you,' I said smiling as the tension dispersed. I then produced the capexs from my laptop case and handed them over.

Roger smiled, 'Like your style.'

He duly signed them and passed them over to Surinder. It was refreshing to see that finance was a function to process, not a department to approve. This is often a blocker, I have found.

Roger turned to Mark Winter, 'I understand we are going to lose one of our biggest customers at this plant; is that correct?'

'Well, they had given us written notification that they were looking to pull away; they were scouting around for another supplier. But we made them an offer to come over and support us in a Kaizen event.'

'Kaizen event, what on?' Mark Lee asked.

'Redesign to cost and putting in a pull Kanban system to ensure 100% on time delivery.'

Mark not only listened but understood what the kaizen event was about.

'Impressive,' Mark Lee commented.

'Good luck with retaining them; I shall be watching with interest on how that will work in practice,' Roger said. 'All eyes are on this site so who knows! If the Kaizen event is a success, we could take it global. Shall we take a tour now, Frank?'

'Sure, no problem!'

We then went on the guided factory tour and by the time we returned to the boardroom all my team were back at their respective departments. I was alone.

'So, Frank,' asked Roger. 'How have you really found it here?'

'Well, it's been challenging but I believe we will get through it; we are already seeing grass roots improvements.'

'Yes, the numbers last month were a lot healthier, is that trend set to continue?'

'Yes,' I said confidently. If you speak with confidence people generally believe you.

Roger started to pack away his belongings, 'We are due to see the other plants now, and Andrew is meeting us at Retford. I believe that's only an hour up the road. Small country!' Roger smiled. 'I will be back in six months' time to see the fruits of your hard work.'

'I look forward to it,' I said.

'Frank, if there's anything you need just holler we're here to help,' Mark Lee declared.

'Thanks, Mark. Much appreciated, but as I say, I've got a good team here.'

'Well, you know where we are,' Mark nodded.

I shook their hands as they left. Once they were out of sight I turned to Helen,

'Thanks for today Helen.'

'You're welcome,' she smiled, 'how do you think it went?'

I watched as the limo drove out of the car-park.

'Very well!' I said, 'very well indeed!' I turned, 'now we have the real job to start.'

I left the reception and headed for the shop floor.

CHAPTER 17

Kaizen Time

The week of the Kaizen event was upon us. We gathered in the training room where I had carefully set out name tags for each of the Kaizen participants. They were formally invited by letter to attend; this makes it official and sets the tone. I placed a saucer by their name tags. Making sure the cups were on the side board next to the coffee and tea urns. Some pastries were also laid out. Helen always does a good job. I attached the laptop onto the projector and waited for the team to appear.

Daniel was first, dressed down in shirt and jeans. I told them all to dress informally and in old clothes as there was going to be a lot of sorting and cleaning to do.

'Daniel, good morning. Now just watch and see what happens.'

'Sure!'

We stood at the front of the table. The team came in and started to congregate by the coffee and teas, each filling their cups with what they desired. Jonty and Pierre had arrived earlier with Fabrizio, and I had already greeted them. Before long the room was buzzing with chatter.

'Now Daniel, watch as they all sit down at their respective places and see what happens to the cups they have in their hands.' Daniel watched intently.

I clapped my hands for their attention, 'OK team can we all sit down and we will begin.' They all responded well and sat in their named seats and every single one of them put the cup on the saucer provided.

'Well done everyone you have now just learnt the basic principle of 5S.' They all looked surprised. 'Everything in its place and place for everything. Each of you sat in the place that was designated to you and all of you without hesitation, put your cup in the right place, which is on the saucer. We are each conditioned to do so. 5S is like that, we should and will do it automatically.'

'Every bin, every pallet, every stillage no matter what, must, and will have their own saucers. Remember that when you come to do the 5S.' All of them nodded in agreement.

'Right, here's the agenda for the whole week,' I continued.

'Introductions will take around forty minutes.' They all looked a little surprised with the amount of time allocated for introduction but that was necessary to do the name game, as I call it.

'We will then have some teaching of Kaizen principles and concepts. Then we will take a break.' There were to be several breaks during the event as it helps people recover and reinvigorate themselves.

'We will have a lunch together.' This is important because it builds a team spirit throughout the week.

'After lunch you will be split into three teams and go to the workplace, the Gemba. Take this time to observe and write down what you see.

'We will return after 40 minutes and use what I call the priority quad.' I showed them the A0 size paper which was on the wall.

'Tomorrow we start earlier, at 8.30am. We will then go to the Gemba and start making things happen. Each team will have a team leader who I have nominated.

Team 1: Daniels team. This team will deal with the 5S of the area.

Team 2: Which I will lead, will deal with the logistics of creating a pull system throughout the factory for these products.

Team 3: Will be led by Fabrizio in looking at the redesign to cost of the product.'

'Your names are on the board as to which team you are going to be in. At 4pm every day we stop. Each member of the team will then present to the rest of the group what they have achieved that day. We will wrap up at 5pm every day. No exceptions!' They all nodded in agreement.

'Do not go back to your desk and start checking your emails. Do not take any calls from anyone during these hours. It is important that you understand the ten rules that govern a Kaizen event.'

Rule 1: For the dedicated person, there is no other responsibility with a higher priority, nor task that takes precedence.

Rule 2: There is no rank within this team. All members are equal.

Rule 3: Keep an open mind to change. If you don't change you will leave yourselves open to be changed.

Rule 4: Change is good; more change is better.

Rule 5: Maintain a positive attitude.

Rule 6: Respect each other.

Rule 7: There is no such thing as a dumb question.

Rule 8: Plans are only good if they can be implemented.

Rule 9: Plans succeed only if the gains are sustained.
Rule 10: There is no substitute for hard work.'

'Any questions so far?'

One of the team members raised his hand. 'What time is lunch?' he asked.

'I thought I said no dumb questions?' we all laughed. '12.30.' I replied.

'On Friday morning each of you will present to the senior team on what we have been doing and what we have achieved in this week.' Some people looked nervous. 'Don't worry we will help you along the way.'

'Now during this long hard week each of you will, at different times, fall into the pit of despair.' They all looked up. 'It's natural, because at some point you will be overwhelmed by the magnitude of the task ahead of you. We, the facilitators, will be there with your team mates to pull you out of the pit.'

I went to the flip chart and wrote my name on it.

'Francis Patrick Walsh' I declared. 'That is the name on my birth certificate. Patrick was my grandfather's name and Francis was my father's name. Walsh comes from my Irish ancestry although I was born in the UK but, as my father used to say, if the bitch has puppies in a stable, it don't make them horses.' They all chuckled at that one.

'So now I want each and every single one of you to come up to the front and write down the name that appears on your birth certificate and explain where it came from.'

What ensued was hilarious, it certainly breaks the ice and people relate to their names and to each other. People who had been working together for years learnt something new about each other. It created a great springboard for the Kaizen event to launch. Hence forty minutes for introductions.

After the name game and much laughter, I wrote on the board.

100% on time in full and 5% reduction in price.

'Right team! That's the goal and we will achieve it in a week.' The smiles faded; some people looked perplexed and some looked like rabbits caught in headlights. I produced a tennis ball.

'Before we start, just one more game. This will make you think about the seemingly impossible task we have ahead of us. So first we will split into two team's right down the middle of the table. Daniel, please get me another tennis ball from the cupboard there would you?' He duly did and I wrote on the board.

'This ball must pass through both of your hands in the quickest time possible.' I handed the ball to the first person on each side of the table.

I passed Daniel a timer, 'please would you time this for me?'

'GO!'

Quickly both teams passed the ball to each other and when it came to the end, we stopped the timer.

'OK, team One. How long?'

'22 seconds,' Daniel declared. This was met with groans.

'Team two?'

'25 seconds,' Daniel said. This too was met with groans and jubilation from team one at the same time.

'Right, that's excellent. Now each of your teams get together and come up with another way of passing the tennis ball between both your hands in a faster time.'

Quickly they all huddled. Some talking and gesturing on how to do it.

'You've got 5 minutes,' I declared. I turned to Daniel and gave him a nod. 'Ready to time it again?'

'Sure!'

Let's give them a minute warning so they can get into position.'

I observed who were the most vociferous in each team and who the quiet ones were (the ones to look out for).

'One minute left!' Daniel declared. Each team formed into a position.

'GO!' I shouted. We timed both teams.

'Finished!' declared team 2.

'12 seconds,' Daniel said.

'14 seconds for team 1.'

I wrote on the board both sets of times for round one and round two.

'Well done teams. Look at the improvements you both made. Just calculate the differences as an improvement as a percentage.'

We did, and there were vast improvements.

'Right, now, I want you to do it in one second.'

I turned to the board and wrote "1 second".

Gasps from the teams! 'That's impossible!' One declared.

'You've got five minutes.'

They all huddled together and the quiet ones now became more vocal.

'One-minute remaining!' declared Daniel.

To my delight both teams formed a Shute by laying their hands-on top of each other. The last person standing on a chair held the tennis ball.

'Go!'

The ball dropped right through the funnel of hands and hit the floor within one second. Delight all round.

As we were congratulating each other I said. 'So, if you are pressed by having a tight target or deadline you think is impossible, you need to think outside the box to overcome it. 25 seconds to just 1 second is impressive; therefore, anything is possible.'

The teams were delighted with themselves so I called a break and they dispersed.

The Kaizen team returned and I put up the Kaizen presentation and talked them through the principles and concepts.

We paused for another break and I turned to Daniel.

'Daniel we now need to put the teams together.' Daniel nodded. We spoke through the names and assigned the people to their teams.

Three teams of four.

The first team was going to do the 5S of the area and the second team was to address the pull vs push systems throughout the factory. The third team was to redesign to cost, taking out as much cost as possible. We took another break and then I explained the process.

'Right teams! In the next stage we are going to the Gemba with our observation boards. I want as many suggestions and observations as we possibly can get. Be critical!

'Before you go all of you please wear the kaizen badges, we have made up for you. This is to ensure that the whole workforce knows who you are and what you doing and that you're not all on time and motion studies.' They laughed; however, it is very important that you communicate to the shop floor what is happening. After all you will be impacting their environment.

'Forty minutes! Back here on time please!' They all left which allowed me to prepare the priority quad section of the event.

When you ask people to come up with as many ideas as they possibly can, you will get a deluge. It's important that each individual feels they have contributed. We have to demonstrate why we are using their ideas and, in some cases, why we are not. The priority quad does just that.

When the teams returned, we debated for around 30 minutes about where to put the posted stickers into which box. Clearly top left (high cost saving quick fix) was going to be the priority and we would put the action plan together to ensure these were done.

All ideas were logged by Daniel so we could address them later on during the year.

'Now know your teams. Your names are allocated to the relevant team leaders.' They all studied the flip chart to find their names.

'Team two will go back to the Gemba and walk the process. Once we have done that, we will put it on the wall with postit stickers representing the current state. We will then brainstorm as to what we would like the future state to be. This will then be mapped and a GAP Analysis performed to produce an action plan to move from the current state to the future state.'

'Team two we want to go from a push system to a pull system. We must introduce Kanban throughout every process. Moving from Push to Pull production has the single greatest impact on improving material flow and eliminating waste.'

'Remember produce only what is ordered, when it is ordered and, in the quantities, required.

The upstream process produces only enough units to replace those that have been withdrawn by the downstream process. Remember the fast-food model!

The six Kanban rules are:

Rule 1: Downstream process withdraws items from upstream process.

Rule 2: Upstream process produces only what has been withdrawn.

Rule 3: Only 100% defect free products are sent to the next process.

Rule 4: Level production must be established.

Rule 5: Kanbans always accompany the parts themselves.

Rule 6: The number of Kanban's are decreased gradually over time.

To calculate your Kanban, use this formula

- Daily output X (lead-time + safety margin) divided by Pallet capacity
- Daily output = Daily output divided by Workdays in month

Manufacturing lead-time (process time + retention time) + lead-time for Kanban retrieval

- Each pallet or container has one Kanban card or sheet
- Kanban cards always accompany the material
- The quantity indicated on the card is the quantity in the container
- Kanban posts hold Kanbans for material that is withdrawn or produced and indicate material that has been used in production

Production Kanbans are placed in production Kanban posts in the same sequence in which the material is withdrawn

- Production occurs in the same order that the production Kanban collects in the production Kanban post.'

'OK team, off you go capture the whole process from start to finish. Then we can spend time working on the pull systems using Kanban.'

I looked at the enthused team. 'Any questions? No? Good! Well look, silence is approval so it's your last chance if you don't understand anything.' A few nods and they were off.

I shouted after them 'Good luck, see you all back here in forty minutes.'

Now to focus on the 5s. I turned to Daniel. 'Right, your team will now start the 5S programme. Let's get the first sort done with red tags. Only red tag any item that is not being used daily by the process. Then I want to introduce you to a Green Tag.'

'Green Tag?' Daniel was bemused.

'Yes, this is for all our hoarders out there. When we red tag we place the tags on items we want to remove from the area so, by default no red tag and the item remains. However, that's too easy, so I introduced a green tag in order that heads of departments must justify why they want the item in the area.'

Daniel expression was wry. I could see he was already working out who would cause issues.

'It's quite powerful. Off you go.'

I left Daniel to it for a while and then decide to take a look at the progress.

'How's the 5S going Daniel?' I asked as I entered the pilot 5S area.

Daniel beamed a big smile. 'Well, we are well on the way with the red tag, sorting all the unnecessary items we don't use anymore, or not required in day-to-day business. Just look at the pile we mustered.'

Daniel walked me into the main hall where there was a pile of items stacked high with red tags attached. 'On the red tags we identified why we felt the items didn't need to be there.

I pick up a red tag and read the reason smiling as I commented, 'an inch of dust is not the excuse really?'

'Only reason we had. So Frank, this new addition of the green tag?' asked Daniel. 'How did that come about?'

'Well, as I said before, if you ask people to identify items for red tags a lot of them will fall to the default position of, I need it.' Daniel nodded. 'If you turn it on its head and ask that within a week's moratorium you must add a green tag to everything you want to keep or it gets removed; it puts the responsibility on the department to justify the items placement.'

'Does it cause problems?'

'Oh yes, there are all sort of issues with reasons to keep it. Some are reasonable but some are totally unnecessary.' One of the Kaizen team approached Daniel and me.

'Excuse me Dan, we've got a problem with Maureen - she's refusing to move one of the cupboards.'

'OK, where is it?' enquired Daniel.

'Over here,' he gestured towards an office and we both followed him. We entered the large office area and standing there was an entrenched Maureen, arms folded.

'What's the issue Maureen?' smiled Daniel.

'This is my stationery cupboard and I use it all the time,' Maureen demanded, 'and they want to take it away from me.' Office Kaizen events are the most emotive of 5S events.

'It's rather a big cupboard Maureen,' Daniel gestured to it.

'It's my stationery cupboard,' Maureen stated.

Daniel looked at me for some guidance so I stepped up and stood at the cupboard.

'Well Maureen, if you use it every day then you can tell me what's in it.'

Maureen looked at me, 'well it's a stationery cupboard so all my stationery,' she declared.

'OK, well it's a large cupboard just to hold paper, pens and paper clips isn't it?' I queried.

'I use it all the time, there's all sorts in there,' Maureen declared.

'OK, so what's actually in here?' I asked again. Silence!

I swung open both cupboard doors to reveal a vacuum cleaner, extension leads and a variety of tools. Admittedly there were paper and pens, and I did spot a large stapler.

Maureen looked surprised and it was clear she hadn't been using it every day.

'Well, the only thing stationery about this cupboard is that's it not moving!' I declared.

We laughed which broke the tension. Some people are natural hoarders and change is difficult but you must be willing to be open to change or you leave yourself open to being changed.

FOOTNOTE TO CHAPTER:

Most 5S implementations fail through management inattention, or leaders delegating their responsibilities to others without support and involvement. Once again, it's down to you the manager. Remember the 5Ms?

There are 10 rules for Office based 5S

1. Nothing on the floor except your feet
2. Nothing on top of filing cabinets and storage cupboards
3. Remove calendars
4. Remove jackets and coats, hi-vis ,etc. from backs of chairs
5. Label each cupboard and filing cabinet
6. Remove filing cabinets not required
7. Personal belongings.
8. Everyone to vet each other's bank of desks and set out a league table. (Maybe reward the best?)
9. In-tray, out tray only
10. Bank all literature (specs catalogues) into a central library

The next stage is to systemize throughout your place of work. Pilot an area to make it look very good and the rest will follow. Nobody really wants to work in a mess. There are many ways to measure your weekly performance and it's important that you do so. Here's an example I find very useful.

5S in not just cleaning up, it's a way of working (WOW) -

it's a culture change. How do you ensure the 5S can be achieved, (sustainability), is by changing the way we do things?

As you move through your operation take extra time to identify the following

No Wandering / No Searching

Everything you need to do a proper job is near at hand and where you left it —and that where you left it is its proper designated place. Shadow boards are a good example of this.

The workplace is clean, well-ordered, self-explaining, and self-regulating. Waste is identified before it accumulates. Material and information flow through the workplace at an accelerated pace. Just think of it as a pit stop in an F1 competition.

Always audit because there is much respect and learning to be gained from auditing. In one case we decided to stop auditing because we trusted the workplace employees to maintain the required high standard and we no longer felt it necessary to audit.

WRONG!

When management ceases to audit and be involved, the workforce will cease to care! That perception will rapidly spread and all the hard work will revert to 'where's my spanner?'

EXAMPLE OF A 5S AUDIT SHEET

		5S Factory Area Self - Audit		eek **ADD IN WEEK NUMB**
			0%	% Score
5S AUDIT (Factory)	Area Name	**NAME OF AREA**		0
	Auditor			

5S	No.	Check Item	Description	Score 1-5
Sort	1	Materials	Are there any unidentified materials lying around in the section?	0
	2	Work / Storage Areas	Are there any unused equipment / racking or other equipment?	0
	3	Tools / Trolleys	Are there any unused tools / trolleys or similar items in the department?	0
	4	Visual Indicators	Is it obvious which items belong to which area and where they should be stored?	0
	5	Work Instructions	Are all standards visual and clearly defined. Are they easily accessible and user friendly?	0
			Sub Total =	0

5S	No.	Check Item	Description	Score 1-5
Set In Order	1	Locations	Are all racking / shop floor areas clearly marked?	0
	2	Components	Do shelves or racks have labels showing which items go where?	0
	3	Safety	Are all walkways and emergency exits clearly marked and free from obstruction?	0
	4	Part Indentification	Are signs or locations used to identify part status?	0
	5	Tools	Are tools stored to facilitate visual picking and returning?	0
			Sub Total =	0

5S	No.	Check Item	Description	Score 1-5
Shine	1	Floors	All floors kept clean and free of waste or debris?	
	2	Storage / Work Areas	Are the storage / work areas cleaned daily and kept free of debris?	
	3	Maintenance	Is there any visual evidence of equipment being maintained on a regular basis?	
	4	Ownership of Area	Is there a person responsible for overseeing the cleaning operations?	
	5	Standard Practise	Do operators sweep floors and clean down at the end of each shift with out being asked?	
			Sub Total =	

5S	No.	Check Item	Description	Score 1-5
Standardise	1	Improvement Ideas	Are improvement ideas being generated monthly?	
	2	Kaizen Activities	Are improvement actions being implemenetd?	
	3	Standard Work	Are standardised procedures written, clear and actively being used?	
	4	CI Process	Is it clear that there is a structured continuous improvement process in place?	
	5	The first 3S's	Are the first three 5's (Sort, Set In order and Shine) being maintained?	
			Sub Total =	0

5S	No.	Check Item	Description	Score 1-5
Sustain	1	Training	Has 5S been incorporated in the induction training programmes for new starters?	
	2	Focus & Awareness	Is 5S reported on at board level, briefed at company communications sessions and supported by senior management?	
	3	People	Is everyone participating in the 5S programme?	
	4	Records	Is a 5S file available and being kept up to date?	
	5	5S Activity Boards	Are activity boards up to date and regularly reviewed by the team?	
			Sub Total =	0

KEY: 1 = BAD   2 = AVERAGE   3 = GOOD   4 = VERY GOOD   5 = WORLD CLASS

FOOTNOTE TO CHAPTER:

7 Steps to Implementation

Reviewing 25 years of observations, the more successful people tend to follow this simple sequence… but that is after setting the Vision, getting the buy-in and identifying a champion. The most senior person should be the sponsor and appoints a champion.

1. Pick a good place to start. One that you know or feel will be successful. This should be an area that you will learn from and that you can replicate and build on its success. Many eyes will be watching. Take it seriously and take many photos of what it looks like before you start. These will be priceless. I always ordered the floor paint and signage weeks in advance of the pilot 5S (as lead times permitted) always a big impact when they turn up on the second day of the brainstorming.

2. Equip the team with the right expectations and tools (5Ms') by giving it unqualified respect and management support. Provide the 5S training needed, ensuring all personnel are involved – production, maintenance, managers and staff. And be sure to give the 'time to learn' to the new processes so self-confidence and pride in doing things differently can grow. The greatest fear for a human being is humiliation and embarrassment, so drive out such fear, as Deming would say.

3. Treat first "S" as a 'waste reduction' activity. Sort out all the things that consume unnecessary thought, effort, and resources. Use cross-functional teams to really get the value of this. Find leakages and hazards and 'Red-tag' every problem. Include an action plan for execution in 20 days.

4. Second "S" is about arranging things. It's the placement and arrangement of equipment and materials. Work teams (with initial training) are freed to execute this.

5. Third "S" means 'shiny clean'. Remember Ford - "We can't afford dirt because it is too expensive!" This one is critical – and must meet an agreed-upon standard – plus, the standard must identify what you need to do to reach it. Everyone in the area must work to the same standard or there is no standard. Again, * be sure to take lots of* photos. You cannot take too many. Remember your shop floor is your showroom.

6. Standardize means - just that - and drive it across the company at a rate that the transformation can be sustained. This is where we make new processes into instinctive habits. Any lukewarm management support here defeats the entire purpose. Incorporate into your WAR (Walk Around Review).

7. Sustain: Where you will spend the rest of your life but not know it because it will have become a habit. The new way of working. Top management's policy

must be free from variation, and take more pictures that will inspire customers as well as employees. Don't hesitate to designate champions for all systems introduced.

The best way to know if 5S has been sustained is when you see something that is abnormal and it jumps out of you, like a crisp packet on a shiny floor or a wrong tool on the shadow board that does not belong. Always remember the saucer for everything has its place and finally, nobody is above 5S.

The ability to sustain 5S will depend on how well management ties and supports expectations to the 'real work' – and to the achievement of full employee involvement. Only through involvement can ownership be developed.

'Visual clutter equates to cluttered thinking' which will generate waste that will cost customers more than they want to pay, or at least cause your selling price to be higher and make your competitive success more vulnerable.

According to the Agility Forum of the 80's and 90's, "Time is the currency of the 21st Century." Add up all the time saved during unscheduled downtime when no time is wasted looking for tools.

5-S is a simple process but it requires discipline to sustain. It is the foundation for the key elements of Lean. It is one of the key foundation stones of 21st Century

Management and must be considered strategically so. It's not just housekeeping or cleaning things up because the 'grown ups' are coming to visit, it's the beginning of world class and without 5S it will always FAIL.

CHAPTER 18

The Art of A3 Thinking

5S Lesson over for now, I left Daniel and the team to it.

My own work stream was to introduce Kanban flow into the process. The first step of this is to value stream. Value-stream mapping usually employs standard symbols to represent items and processes; therefore, knowledge of these symbols is essential to correctly interpret the production system problems.

Value-stream mapping is a lean-management method for analysing the current state and designing a future state. It visualizes the series of events that take a product or service from its beginning through to the customer with reduced lean wastes as compared to the current map. A value stream focuses on areas of a firm that add value to a product or service, whereas a value chain refers to all of the activities within a company.

I find the best way to start a value stream map is to walk the process and then brown paper process map the steps.

By visually mapping out, in a simple way, the steps in the process, the team can start to see constraints and add improvement steps. Most importantly, the team can spot opportunities for removing and reducing waste in the process. However, as this particular work stream was about introducing Kanban principles the focus was to be where we could make the changes while considering the upstream and downstream process impacts.

While my team were working through some issues, I left them to it and went to find Fabrizio to see how he was doing with his task which I had quickly briefed him on earlier. He had to take cost out of the product and this required him to start with a complete cost breakdown using an A3 scoping document. I had shown him the A3 report and an example document:

A3 reports are meant to be used as a team problem solving tool; they ask the right questions in the correct way. The root cause analysis must be undertaken with a cross functional team and the solution should match the problems.

It is a powerful tool and I spent time with Fab going through the process. He had studied it for a while and understood the concept.

A3 Report

(c) Sigma Magic

Title: A3 Report Title

Team: Team Members

Last Updated: 26 05 2013 19:17

Background	Counter Measures			
Initial Condition	**Implementation Plan**			
	Item	Resp	Due Date	Status
Target Condition	**Issues / Follow-up Actions**			
Root Cause Analysis	**KPI Metrics**			
	Metric	Baseline	Goal	Current

'Get cost breakdowns on key products and components. Look at the bill of materials if possible and don't forget to gather drawings and technical specifications, including marketing requirements if applicable. Invite the opinion of the design engineering representatives.'

Fab had nodded; he clearly knew what was expected but I needed to ensure it was team work and not just him. 'Make sure Pierre and Jonty are involved all along the way.'

'Of course, they're my friends.' That was the last thing I heard from him as he led his team to a break-out room.

I placed my hand on the door handle of his break-out room but could hear lively debate and discussion happening so I chose not to interrupt the creative flow. Sometimes it's about knowing when to leave the team to it.

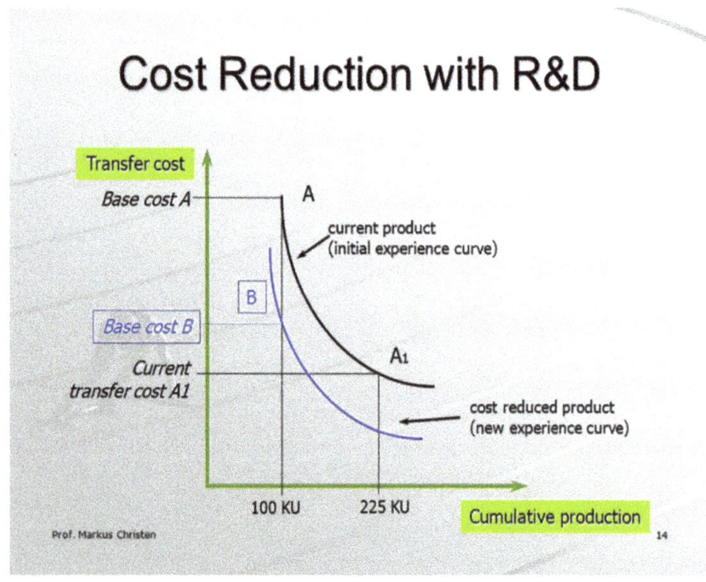

After a week of hard work, the Kaizen task was done.

The Friday presentation was organized and we were to present to Andrew and the Executive Leadership Team with the addition of all the other site managers. We had sparked some interest and the stage was set. The boardroom had a buzz about it as we walked in and the audience were ready, anticipating success.

I introduced the teams and what their objectives were for the week. That was my only participation in the presentation. It's important to step back and allow the team to shine; to take ownership of their activities.

Daniels team went first on organization of the workplace area and 5S. He explained what he and his team had achieved and was very visual with 'before and after' photographs. It's very important that you take as many 'before,' photos as possible and then from the same spot take the 'after', photos.

His team then moved on to showing the new cleaning stations and I was pleased to hear from one of the team members, 'when we put the cleaning stations in, we made sure they were on saucers!'

Finally, they demonstrated the sustainability of the process with audit sheets and cleaning schedules. The place looked and felt a hundred times better and I was particularly proud of Daniel; he had grown so much in confidence and was learning all the time.

Next up was the value stream mapping Kanban presentation. They had put in a system throughout the plant to pull the finished goods product and all the downstream processes it required.

They clearly defined the Runner, Repeaters and Stranger's methodology and ran through the Kanban rules. They showed the Kanban cards they had designed and delivered. Safety stocks were a bit higher than I wanted but I thought it was a good starting point.

Then Fabrizio and his team presented. They declared through redesign and alternative procurements on component parts that they had taken 9.5% costs out of the existing product. After conceding a 5% initial price reduction that meant the customer received a further 2.5%. That was 7.25% total cost reduction for the customer and 2.5% for us.

When the presentations were complete a spontaneous applause erupted from the audience. The atmosphere in the room was one of success and positivity.

When the pleasantries were completed, I took all the team out for fish and chips as a thank you and in celebration of the work they had all achieved.

Remember Kaizen concept seven?

Celebrate achievements!

CHAPTER 19

The Appraisal System

I was finding my time in the plant enjoyable now. I did my daily rounds and remained a supportive presence to the team. However, there were still tasks to be completed here; my work was far from finished as I would discover when a flustered Paula entered the office.

'Frank, I need your help. We've got to get the appraisals completed by November,' she announced.

'How does this usually pan out?' I enquired.

'Not good! I guess that's why the Henderson scores were all bad. Worst in the global company.'

'So, what's the point in doing it? Sounds like a stick to hit people with,' I commented.

'Well, it's the governance - the grown-ups need to see it done,' she said, trying to justify it.

'Tick box exercise then,' I declared.

'Afraid so!' She placed the appraisals forms down onto the table.

I picked up the forms and started to read them. It was clear these were ill thought out and were not really going to achieve anything. The usual backward thinking traditional appraisal system; not the most inspiring process and far too subjective, which was why most people dreaded it.

'What was the HR plan as a direct result of the information fed back to the management last year?'

'There wasn't one. We went into the black hole so it went by the wayside.'

Exasperated I sat down, I was not surprised but I thought it sounded familiar. The best book I read on this was Jack Welch's autobiography and it made me stop the above practice and start a new one.

In a recent Human Resources Forum poll,16% of the people responding had no performance appraisal system at all. Supervisory opinions provided once a year are the only appraisal process for 56% of the respondents. Another 16% described their appraisals as based solely on supervisors' opinions but administrated more than once a year.

'I have seen this everywhere I have worked. The usual reaction from the senior staff is, "Oh no, it's not that time of year again!'

'When they do get around to it, it's invariably rushed, ill prepared and not at all constructive. Then, when completed, it's put back into the HR file and forgotten about until the following year.' Paula nodded in agreement so I continued. 'Unnecessary repetition. Every year the differential between the highest grade and the lowest grade get wider and wider with no end in sight. How can that be fair?'

Paula spoke, 'it isn't fair but that's the way it is. How do we change it Frank?'

I stood up and walked over to my whiteboard and wiped it clean ready to explain an appraisal system I truly believe adds value to the process. Paula sat back in her chair ready to hear what I had to say.

'In my opinion grading systems by seniority and longevity never works and can be very divisive. For many years I have been using a method which ensures a *fair* procedure for all, awarding pay increases, eliminating the grading system. My method is about measuring the person not the job. It's not a new problem it goes back years; we devised the 4A Appraisal System in 1999 at a heavily unionized company with a lot of friction between its members.

I write 4A on the whiteboard and continue;

'It seemed like an impossible task at the time but I put a task force together consisting of shop stewards from unions, senior management, office administration and the shop floor (each area being represented.) My brief was clear. Make it fair! It took six weeks and a private ballot to implement and is a success story I'm very proud of.'

'How did it work?' Paula asked.

'So, it was called the 4A Appraisal System,' I said nostalgically. 'It combines; Attendance, Ability, Adaptability and Attitude. Each were measured on a scale of 4 (4 X 4 = 16) once all four scores were added up, they fell within these categories:' I start to list them out:

If the score was between 0-4 there would be an HR Training and a Personal Improvement Plan required for the individual.

Score between 5-10 you would get the Standard % cost of living, pay increase.

Score 11-14 - Above % cost of living pay increase

Score 14-16 - Bonus highest level then would become mentors.'

Paula interrupted me, 'How do you truly measure these though?'

'Good question: the 4A's were broken down as follows; Attendance: Very emotive but we only dealt with the cold facts here. You scored 4 if you were 100% on time and in attendance. No exceptions; so, if you were unfortunate enough to break a leg then that was not the only bad break you had; you also you got a break in attendance.'

Paula pulled a grim face at this but I continued.

'It's meant to be fair, Paula; there are always exceptions of course, like maternity leave or other personal reasons, but we have to be strict or it becomes subjective again.

The other factor of attendance was timekeeping; therefore, arriving on time for your shift meetings or being at your machine dead on the time you were allocated. Also, the drifting in and out of the tea room and the number of comfort breaks taken during the course of the day. This also applied to meetings.'

'How did you roll it out?' enquired Paula.

'The procedure starts with the 4A assessments. These are done on a one-to-one basis and the scores signed off by both parties once they agree. Then the assessment is sent to HR for processing. If there are disagreements in the scores then arbitration was enacted with representatives from the Unions and Staff. I would only deal with exceptions or appeals.'

'I see. hHw do you measure Ability?' Paula asked.

'Based on the skills matrix then this drove the I L U O training model"

I   Needs supervision for operating

L   No supervision required for operating

U   Set up and operating

O   Mentor. Trainer.

'As a % of competency you were awarded points, the same as for attendance. If, in your area, you could operate every machine and complete all administration duties (including the IT systems you needed) and of course all the necessary documentation you achieved a 4.

Assessment Criteria	
Score 1 = 0-45% of skills in area achieved	
Score 2 = 46-75% of skills in area achieved	
Score 3 = 76-90% of skills in area achieved	
Score 4 = 91-100% of skills in area achieved	

	= 1 Point
	= 2 Points
	= 3 Points
	= 4 Points
●	= 5 Points

% Skills score =

$$\frac{\text{Number of skills achieved + Score for each skill}}{\text{Total Possible Score}} \times 100$$

Total Possible Score = (Total Number of Skills on Matrix) X 5

'Ok I get that. What about the next element?' asked Paula.

'Right so, Adaptability– the definition of how good a person is at fitting into new circumstances, situations, etc.'

Measured on two elements

1) Speed of learning new skills and adapting to new working methods
2) Flexibility

Assessment Criteria
Score 1 = Achieving (achieved) no skills
Score 2 = Achieving (achieved) skills slower than expected time and struggling to adapt to new ways of working
Score 3 = Achieving (achieved) skills within expected time and adapting to new ways of working
Score 4 = Achieving (achieved) skills quicker than expected time and quickly adapting to new ways of working

1 = Unsatisfactory Below Average
2 = Adequate
3 = Satisfactory
4 = Excellent

2. Flexibility

Positive Examples	Negative Examples
Is prepared to change shifts and jobs	Is unwilling to change shifts and jobs
In case of reorganisation, he/she is prepared to take up a part of the redistributed task.	Is angry when has to work on a different project or machine, after a normal training period
Is prepared to adapt to a new supervisor/manager	Always finds a reason not to adapt
Has a wide range of skills and learns quickly	Has limited skills and is slow to learn
Is prepared to work overtime when required	Will not work overtime

Score 1 = Achieving (achieved) no skills

Score 2 = Achieving (achieved) skills slower than expected time and struggling to adapt to new ways of working

Score 3 = Achieving (achieved) skills within expected time and adapting to new ways of working

Score 4 = Achieving (achieved) skills quicker than expected time and quickly adapting to new ways of working

'OK got that. What about measuring attitude?' Paula asked, sitting forward in her chair and engaging in this new appraisal system.

'Yes, sometimes the hardest to quantity as it can be subjective. So, I broke it down into a list.'

1) Health & Safety
2) Communication
3) Team working
4) Attitude
5) Learning new things
6) Problem solving
7) Working independently
8) Taking initiative
9) Productivity
10) Practical approach to performing tasks
11) Quality
12) Housekeeping

'We have to be careful about the budget here Paula so we have some rules. Simply, whatever your budget % is, then that's your bucket of funds so once you get your scores in you can calculate what are the standard % and the above standard % to be. You do not spend over the budget but while maintaining fiscal stability you reward and recognize the stars.'

Here are some typical examples of appraisal score sheets.

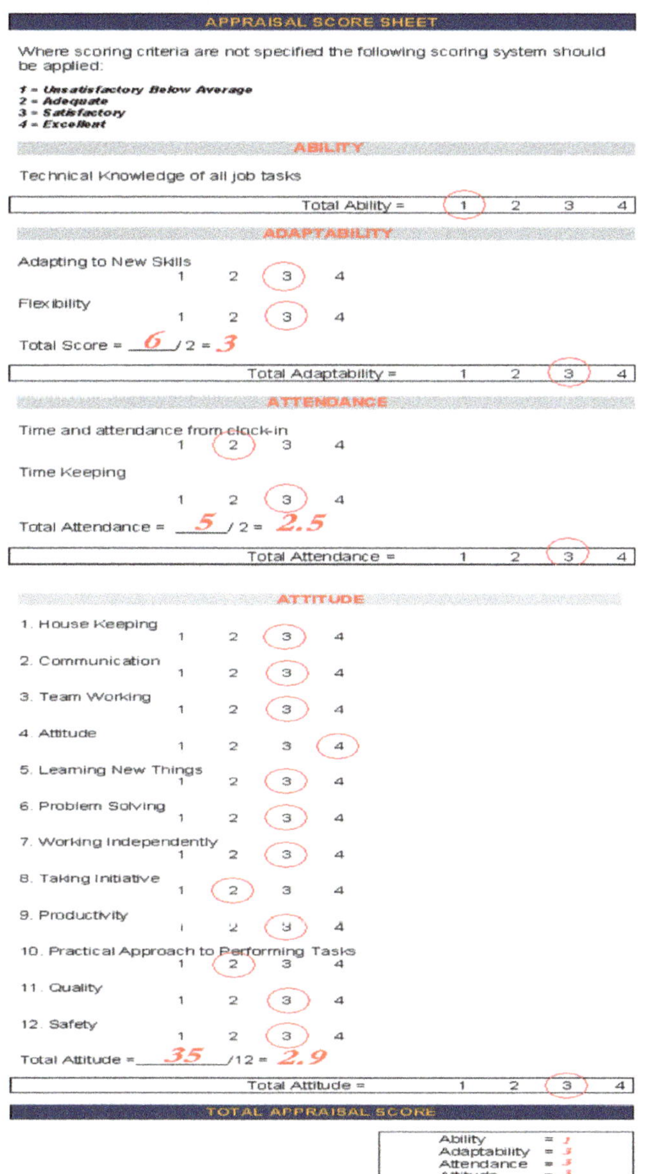

APPRAISAL SCORE SHEET

Where scoring criteria are not specified the following scoring system should be applied:

1 = Unsatisfactory Below Average
2 = Adequate
3 = Satisfactory
4 = Excellent

ABILITY

Technical Knowledge of all job tasks

Total Ability =   (1)   2   3   4

ADAPTABILITY

Adapting to New Skills
1   2   (3)   4

Flexibility
1   2   (3)   4

Total Score = __6__ / 2 = 3

Total Adaptability =   1   2   (3)   4

ATTENDANCE

Time and attendance from clock-in
1   (2)   3   4

Time Keeping
1   2   (3)   4

Total Attendance = __5__ / 2 = 2.5

Total Attendance =   1   2   (3)   4

ATTITUDE

1. House Keeping
1   2   (3)   4

2. Communication
1   2   (3)   4

3. Team Working
1   2   (3)   4

4. Attitude
1   2   3   (4)

5. Learning New Things
1   2   (3)   4

6. Problem Solving
1   2   (3)   4

7. Working Independently
1   2   (3)   4

8. Taking Initiative
1   (2)   3   4

9. Productivity
1   2   (3)   4

10. Practical Approach to Performing Tasks
1   (2)   3   4

11. Quality
1   2   (3)   4

12. Safety
1   2   (3)   4

Total Attitude = __35__ / 12 = 2.9

Total Attitude =   1   2   (3)   4

TOTAL APPRAISAL SCORE

Ability	= 1
Adaptability	= 3
Attendance	= 3
Attitude	= 3

Frank Walsh

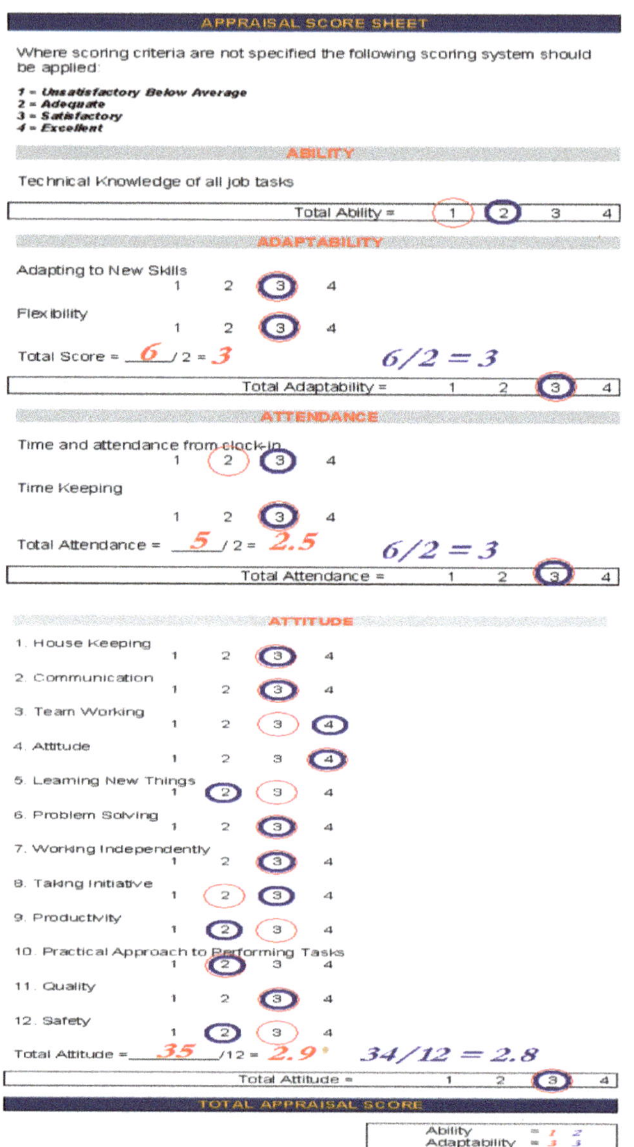

'We did this experiment with two people: Mickey and Ray. The contrast was exactly what the 4A was designed to reveal. Ray had been at the company most of his life and Mickey had been there eight years, but there was a significant gap in their pay rates which Mickey was well aware of.

Ray scored 80% on attendance so he got 3, but only achieved 10% on ability which scored 1. He had adaptability marked at 10% so scored 1, which reflected on his attitude which at 40% scored 2. This equalled a 7 on the scorecard.

Mickey had 100% attendance scoring 4. 40% ability scored 2. 50%, adaptability scored 2. 90% attitude scored 3, equalling 11 on the scorecard.

Therefore, Ray got 5% increases whereas Mickey deservedly received 7%. At this rate the injustice that had befallen Mickey would be narrowed in 3 short years.

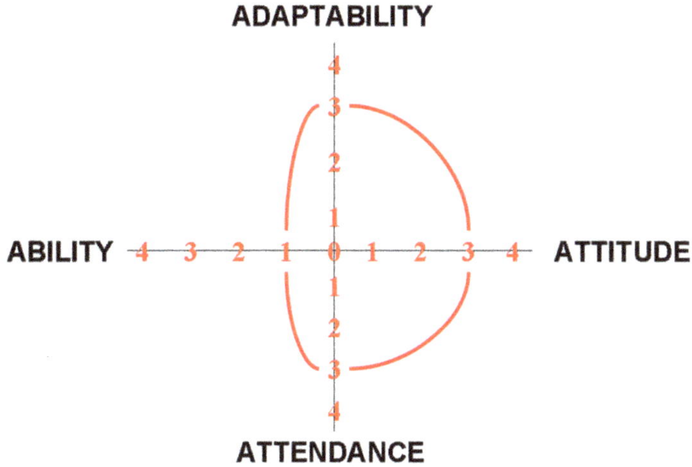

'But what if they all score high?' asked Paula.

'Then you reward them all fairly. If you have all your employees at 16 then you as a business can afford them more money because your business is thriving. However, high marks are hard to come by if administrated correctly.' I continued, 'It's amazing the impact that fairness makes and the trust it engenders.'

'Yes, that is true,' agreed Paula.

'Oh also, lets change the annual schedule. Going forward we should diary in at least one appraisal a month to each and every one of our direct reports. Mutually agree the time and stick to it no matter what; it's more important than board meetings.'

'erm… that's a lot of people Frank.'

'Well Paula, I put it to you that a well-motivated loyal employee is worth more than a well-oiled and productive machine which you spend a lot of time daily and weekly maintaining, and you may have a lot of them. Of course, it's going to take time and effort, but remember your employees are your competitive edge.'

'Yes, that's true; I just don't think everyone sees it that way, do they?' Paula challenged.

'Not everyone. Not yet. That must change. What does this indicate to your direct reports? It shows how important they are to you; it values them and makes them feel valued. You have to be fresh and alert and never have a desk between you and your team member. It needs to be two way and open. Prepare all your paperwork and allocate 30 minutes to 2 hours maximum per person. You can flex this depending on individuals, but for most people really, just 10 minutes is enough for them to remember the measures.'

The whiteboard becomes the list and I underlined as I wrote the important points. I added the 2pm rule to the growing number of points raised.

'Remember, two ears but only one mouth, so use them in that proportion. After the assessment develop the 4A on the area requiring improvement. Praise the areas of improvement, then agree the next steps in their own improvement plan, reminding them not to commit to anything they cannot deliver.'

'What happens if they only score four?' Paula asked.

'Then a Performance Improvement Plan is required. It needs to be followed through at regular intervals, at a minimum once a quarter. Managers and supervisors need to keep to the commitment of the PIP including the time needed away from the job, payment for courses agreed upon, and work assignments.

'Also, this requires HR support and we must not forget that.'

I smiled and nodded, 'yes, of course, it goes without saying. Hopefully we won't have too many people who need that level of support. The point is that this whole process makes the annual review so much easier but you will also have a solid relationship with your team, I guarantee it. Calculate what that really means for you in time per month.'

I drew the calculation on the board to show my point.

'Right, how many Direct Reports do you have?'

Paula takes a moment to consider the question, 'Eight across the group.'

'So, if the average is 30 minutes that's X 12. That's around four hours per month. How many days a year does that represent? So, in one working year that's the time you spend talking directly to your direct staff. Not too much to ask out of 230 working days is it?

'No, not at all when you look at it like that. I still don't know how we could roll this out though?'

'Then we need some HR support to formulate it into a companywide development plan to be budgeted based on this, the annual appraisals always need to be processed before the budget preparation begins so you have the funds to keep your stars.'

Paula nodded, 'I agree, but we need to plan it. There's nothing worse than raising expectations and then letting your most valuable assets down by not following through.'

'There are three rules of management,' I declared. 'Follow up, follow up and follow up.'

'But it's a cost so it will need to be considered, especially if you're talking about training and development costs as an ongoing investment,' Paula declared.

'One per cent of turnover of sales is not much to ask for the training and development of your most vital assets.

Your people! What's your 1% turnover? Fifty million pounds, so £400,000 should be the training budget. What's your current training budget?'

Paula cringed as she told me, '£30,000.'

'Well, that's £127 per head per annum!'

Paula paused and reflected, 'I never saw it like that. What about the bonus schemes?'

'Most contracts will provide for some basic monetary payment but many introduce the concept of a bonus payment. This is a bonus in addition to the normal basic payment, but why? For what reasons?

'Bonuses are paid for a number of reasons. They usually reflect some performance or act on the part of an individual or group of employees.

'In order to improve attendance, some companies will reward those employees who achieve high or perfect attendance but there is always a danger that such a scheme could be discriminatory against employees who have a recognized disability.

'As we know, many bonuses are paid on the performance of the individual, their work out-put, sales performance, or paid to a group of employees who have performed well. Again, this can create a problem with discrimination where an employee is absent through sickness or perhaps on maternity leave.'

'So how does that work with the first A - attendance if you have a baby?

'Well, everything is discretionary of course but we have to be fair across the board. Let's just be sensible about it, but generally no attendance means no attendance.'

I continued, 'maternity, even paternity and bereavement absence, shouldn't be included in the attendance score.'

'Bonuses are paid because of the performance of the company or organization. They are usually based on the profitability and some form of calculation is used to determine the amount of money that will be available to distribute among the staff. Such bonuses, though, can create difficulties about when they are paid, who is entitled, and if the employees have to be in employment at the time of payment. Don't get me wrong Paula, bonuses are a wonderful idea in principle to reward staff, but they are edged with potential pitfalls where equality, discrimination and less favourable treatment can creep into the equation. You have to be mindful of this.'

'What impact does non-payment have on the morale of the staff?' asked Paula.

'Bonuses are an incentive required to keep good people with you. Talented people are rare and you must keep them. I always try to link their bonuses on enhanced performance, not just by hitting the fiscal budgets because that's what they're paid their salaries for.'

I pause for a moment, and recall a situation I faced a while back.

'Maurice Edwards, senior buyer, only scored a 12 and received the standard % bonus, so out of a potential £8k he received £960. He was livid!'

'Did he leave?' she asked.

I continued, 'A few weeks later I summoned him into my office and asked him to go that very afternoon to Brazil. A major supplier had let us down and I needed a guy I could trust to be on the ground for me. He obliged and left that afternoon for what turned out to be a 30-hr. round trip.'

'Wow that's commitment!' Paula commented.

'In his weeks absence I sent a bunch of flowers to his wife and a basket of Easter eggs for their three children, (as it was the Easter holiday at the time) stating on the card, the company thanks you for supporting him while he supports the company". He speaks of that gesture to this day and the 12% is never raised; in fact, is forgotten.'

'I see; so monetary bonuses are not the only answer?'

'Exactly, I have found most people really want recognition rather than just a financial reward.'

'But the sales force is treated differently!' Paula announced. She really was becoming a worthy challenger of my ideas and I cherished her opinion.

'Yes, bonuses are a complex and sometimes divisive concept. There seems to be a lot of inequality to them. Sales, budgets, commission, etc. seems to be out of kilter with standard bonuses. I'm told this is to keep the best sales people motivated?'

'Yes, they seem to be a different type of beast,' Paula said.

'If salespeople are awarded bonuses on a target number of orders acquired in a given month, they may feel that orders received over the target figure would be of greater benefit to them if they were to be held over to the following month to ensure that that month's target is also met.'

'Really!' Paula declared. 'What effect does that have?'

'Well, it puts more pressure on the operation to perform as there is no 'visibility' of this order until the beginning of the new month. Also, the customer requires it for that month. I have known salespeople to move into the following month to protect their bonuses. It really does drive the wrong behaviour.'

'It does! They should be audited to stop that.'

'Maybe! It has a knock-on effect. Procurement is not given the information so cannot negotiate a good volume break price; manufacturing will have to do more set ups. The list goes on, but if they had had visibility they could have processed at the same time. Suppliers would have to re-ship raw material when they could have done so in bulk. There are many impacts on the overall efficiency of the plant as a direct result of the wrong KPI.'

'How do we change this paradigm without using bonuses then?' Paula asked.

'It is difficult and needs courage. A concept growing these days is a bonus scheme broken down into three parts. Companywide Targets, Departmental Targets, Individual Targets. This concept deals with the Companywide Targets: if they have been achieved then everyone in a management bonuses scheme (MBS) receives a percentage of their allocated bonus. After all everyone must have contributed to the success. If the Departmental Targets are achieved a further percentage is awarded.

If Individual targets within that department are achieved or exceeded, then a further percentage bonus is awarded. Therefore no one in the MBS can achieve any bonus at all if the company itself (as an entity) does not achieve budgeted targets.

The individual bonuses within the department will each receive a further enhancement if they achieve their own budget target but if an individual doesn't, but the department does achieve, then that individual should only receive the companywide and departmental proportion of the bonuses. This is supported by using the 4As appraisals system.

What does this do? Firstly, driven by the necessity to achieve bonuses it will drive departments to work closer together for the 'common goal'. It will create an environment of transparency and build a teamwork approach to problems.

Bonus payments can, with proper consideration, be excellent motivational tools to a workforce; they can also be divisive if one group feels that its efforts are not properly rewarded compared to another group. When you are considering implementing such schemes, involve the employees to gain their views. In a larger organization you might consider having a small work group that assists with the development and monitoring of bonus schemes within the workplace.

Used wisely bonus schemes are excellent ways of rewarding employees and can be a factor in recruitment and retention of staff; however, if they are not kept under review they can lead to discontent and potential discrimination claims. That's why the 4As are a good methodology to adopt.

I take a breath and Paula is sitting back, thinking about the plan. 'OK Frank, I agree!' Paula declared. 'Doesn't it create more work though, more paperwork? More red tape?'

'Not at all. We need to get away from layers of reports and red tape. By the way, the term "red tape" was borne out of the American civil war when soldiers from both sides were expected to go to Washington DC to collect their war pensions. Many would travel hundreds of miles and once there they would sometimes wait for days while the administration located and filed their records. Each soldier received a scroll of paper tied up with red tape and that's where the saying comes from.'

'I didn't know that,' Paula said.

'Invariably annual pay negotiations and bonuses are never really challenged as it's in the 'too difficult' pile. Look at the damage it really does to a business. Worth thinking about.'

Paula nodded in agreement.

'Let's do the appraisals, but let's do it based on facts and the 4As.'

'Let's!' declared Paula.

CHAPTER 20

Time to Go

The daily disciplines of the DMS and the lockdown were starting to show results. No time wasting in meetings and I created a site leadership team meeting whereby the leadership team would meet once a fortnight. The agenda was simple. We would all meet for ninety minutes once every two weeks. The rest of their time was spent working on their four tasks and I also ensured that each of the department heads were working on initiative's which would drive OTIF.

Each department would then present on four slides only, to the rest of the senior team, SLT as it became known. It wasn't a talking shop it was a presentation of what their respective departments had achieved. I saw myself in the leadership role as the conductor of an orchestra, making sure harmony existed within the orchestra pit. I made sure I didn't play any of the instruments – that was their job.

When we all met, thirty minutes of the ninety were dedicated to an Area Safety Inspection. ASI. We would all meet and assign two groups to walk the Gemba (and be seen to do so by everyone) and make an independent area safety inspection. When we arrived back at the boardroom, we would then highlight any safety issues or hazardous conditions which were fixed on the spot or certainly within the following twenty-four hours. It was fast and effective and showed the whole workforce that we took ASI very seriously. Chris McAteer, the union rep was also invited to the SLT and the ASI. His objectivity and focus were valuable and gave credibility to the whole process.

Weeks became months. The daily discipline of the management system generated the much-needed improvement. Systems are one thing but it's the people that are key. However, I was the conductor and I was becoming restless. My work here was almost done and I made some adjustments, I had one more recommendation which I was personally going to execute. One morning, I asked Daniel to come to my office. Paula Bartram was in attendance.

'You wanted to see me boss?' he beamed. Always smiling, always upbeat. He noticed Paula and nodded to her.

'Yes, come in please sit down. I asked Paula to sit in on this meeting because I wanted to give you some advice about the management of people.'

'Why? Have I done something wrong?' His smiled dropped.

'No, no, not at all,' I reassured him and his smiled returned.

'As a leader you should be seen. Make your presence felt. Connect with staff; don't just lock yourself in your office the whole day and only communicate with staff when you want something done. Get to know your employees. Find out about their interests.'

'I'm never in my office now; I've got time as I don't spend my day bogged down with emails. Only seven this morning,' confirmed Daniel. I was happy he was still following the disciplines I'd showed him so I continued;

'Showing employees that you genuinely care is a skill, Daniel. If an employee is dealing with an issue, whether personally or professionally, show empathy. Advocate for your team and stand up for them; don't throw your people under the bus when things go wrong.'

'Yes, I remember the phone call that we were supposed to be having that Sunday when you said, "Bog off!"' I smiled and nodded in appreciation.

'Practice open and honest two-way communication. Keep employees informed; don't let them have to hear of upcoming changes through the grapevine. Listen to employees; have an atmosphere where employees' ideas and suggestions are valued.'

'I want you to be fair and neutral. Treat everyone fairly; don't pick favourites; lead by example. Be known as a person of integrity.'

'I try my best, Frank.'

'I know you do. I've been observing you over the past few months and if there's one thing you cannot teach it's integrity, and you have got it in bundles.'

'Empower Employees. Provide them with the proper tools then give them room to get the job done. Don't micromanage!'

'Five M's; I know.' Daniel said.

'Reward and Recognition; offer incentives to show employees how much you value and appreciate them. Always reward staff for good work and not only top performers, include those who are improving or doing their best. Be generous with a "Thank You." Small tokens of appreciation like supermarket voucher schemes. Every month someone should get something for going the extra mile.

'Yes, it goes down very well.'

'People really only want to be recognized, not so much rewarded,' I said.

'Recommend employees for training and new opportunities. Staff members can interpret an employer's unwillingness to invest in training as a disregard for their professional development. Acknowledge and encourage strengths; recognize the different skills they possess and recommend training and development opportunities.'

'Yes, I will. I know what it's like to be developed and the benefits that ensue.'

'That's why I am recommending you to be the next Operation Manager of the plant.'

Daniel's jaw dropped with shock as I quickly ran through some new terms and conditions, including an increase in salary, bonus scheme and the other perks.

'Congratulation's son!' I put my hand out and Daniel tearfully shook it, then spontaneously hugged me. 'Well deserved! Well done!' I patted him on the back.

'Thank you so much!'

'Right,' I pulled away. 'You need to think about your first 100 days in charge. I want to see just four things that you are going to complete.'

'Yes, I totally get it and I know what I need to do,' Daniel said excitedly and he left the room with the stride of someone who was heading places.

'That was nice,' Paula said.'

'Nothing more than he deserves,' I replied. 'At least he will continue with what we have put in place.'

'Yes,' she said, 'we don't want another Operations Manager coming in and dismantling everything you've put in place.'

'Precisely! He is well respected and they all work well as a team,' I smiled to myself and felt very happy for him. The last rule of 5S is sustainability and this is often the hardest part of transformation and improvement.

The last thing we need is to have a return to the old way of doing things. Generally, the people who contributed to the downfall will revert back to type. Staying in their offices building kingdoms and not going to the Gemba where the money is made and where the work gets done.

People and processes are linked. I see clearly that the more a business changes processes and not people the better it becomes. Moving Daniel into the Operations Manager position ensured that the new way of working would continue and therefore sustain all the good work that had been done by the team. As we reached the six-month marker the Americans returned as they said they would. This time Andrew and the rest of the executive leadership team were present. This was to be my last meeting with them all. I was looking forward to having the Henderson employee survey results, too, as they were due out and I hadn't seen or heard the results yet. The boardroom was full when I walked in with the site leadership team. We all sat down. Roger Rewinkle headed the table and started to speak in his southern drawl.

'Thank you all for attending today. Can I start by saying what an amazing turnaround you and your team have brought about in this Plant? In summary,' he continued, 'the operational issues with the poor implementation of the new ERP system highlighted our weaknesses and this resulted in poor performance. We had seriously damaged customer relationships and there was poor employee morale. Within three months on all key metrics there were noticeable improvements, notably around customer care and operational performance. You have beaten the sales budget by 11% and waste reduction by 25%. In the last eight months you have increased "on time delivery" to our customers from 56% to 94%. Your EBIDTA projection was to be a minus £600k but you made a £30k profit. That's a swing of over £2 million from the projection in the first quarter. In that time, you have also reinstated all the necessary outside quality accreditations to continue trading. Also in that period, customer complaints have halved.'

I looked around the room there were a lot of beaming smiles and nods of acknowledgment, Roger continued,

'You have also retained your number one customer which is a £7 million account. This was mainly because of the amazing Kaizen event you orchestrated in the second quarter of this year.

'My understanding is that you have successfully delivered uninterrupted, 100% on time to them since the pull system was put into play. Your plant here also received the best improved supplier award from them as a result.'

Roger opened the A4 brown envelope revealing the Henderson results. 'All this and improving employee morale using the output from the employee survey which we need to be mindful was anonymous. The participation level of the survey was 84%, the highest in this plant ever. What the Henderson survey shows us is a year-on-year improvement by 25 points, the biggest single improvement in any of the global companies for which we are responsible.'

He continued, 'And more importantly you have left a foundation for growth in the next fiscal year and a solid team that will sustain all the improvements you have made.' Roger paused, he took off his glasses and looked directly at me. I felt my spirits lift in response to the amazing results of the engagement survey.

'Frank, and your team, that's a job well done!' Roger turned to Andrew, 'it's amazing to think how you managed to do all this so quickly'. Andrew bowed his head.

'Frank, I'd like a quick word with you afterwards if you don't mind.'

I looked up surprised, 'Yes of course!'

Roger then turned to the room.

'Thank you for all your efforts and work here: a really remarkable turnaround.' Roger gestured to the boardroom and slowly everyone stood up and left the room.

When they had all gone Roger stood up and went over to the coffee machine, 'Coffee Frank?'

'Please,' I replied.

'Frank that has been an incredible job of a turnaround. That's true leadership!'.

'Thank you!'

Roger placed a coffee in front of me and sat down.

'How would you feel about staying on full time?'

I was surprised.

It's what this business needs; someone who gets results, and more importantly, the manner in which they are achieved.' He looked at the empty chair which Andrew normally occupied.

'Thank you, but it's not for me.'

Roger looked back at me. 'We were led to believe that these results were due to you locking down the business and not allowing anyone in to interfere and help.'

'Yes, that's true,' I said.

'We were also led to believe you ruled with an iron fist, autonomous in your approach and brutal in your execution, to ensure rapid results.'

I was aghast and Roger could see it. 'However, the Henderson survey results clearly show that this is not the case and that we have been misinformed.'

'Clearly misinformed!' I spluttered.

Roger raised his hand, 'I know! It is clear! The foundation stones have been laid for a solid performance next fiscal year.'

I was reassured but I was wondering why anyone would tell Roger that? The fox came to mind.

'Frank I am not going to allow this business to fall back into bad ways. It is clear the ERP system has been the excuse all along when clearly it was just down to the leadership from the very top.' I sat in silence. 'As we speak Andrew is being dismissed.'

"This is not because of you or anything you and your team has done. Let me tell you something Frank, that I have learned over many years.'

'I have never fired anyone in my life, they have brought it on themselves, and I resent them putting me in the position where I have to fire them.' Roger raised his finger, 'Remember that!' he said sternly. 'Besides, we have a duty of care to Andrew; he is not performing across all the sites and is beginning to show signs of stress and anxiety. He will be OK! He will find his niche and be happier for it.'

I nodded, it was true, Andrew had lost his passion and his integrity.

'Frank, I'd have liked you to consider staying on but I respect your decision.' I understand that when things are working well you would become bored and then unhappy unless we could offer you a role big enough to keep you occupied.' Roger smiled and I was impressed at how quickly he had understood me despite my only having met him three times in ten months.

'What will you do now?' he asked.

'Nothing! A little holiday and a well-earned rest I think.'

'Well, you deserve it,' Roger put out his hand. 'Thanks Frank, a hell of a job.'

I shook his hand, stood up and took my leave.

I entered my office and some of the teams were there.

Daniel asked, 'you staying boss?'

I looked over at Mark, Scott and Paula.

'Afraid not Daniel.' Daniel's smile disappeared very quickly.

'Why boss?' he asked.

'Well Daniel, an interim is like a dentist,' I explained, 'I've been working as an interim consultant for over 15 years now and I've had the pleasure of working with some great companies and fantastic people. I enjoy the variety; whether it's making sausages or tanks it's all about processes. I've worked in automotive, aerospace, print and packaging, HVAC and medical.'

'There's one common thread throughout all my assignments and I liken it to being a dentist!'

'A dentist?' Daniel laughed.

'No one likes going to the dentist; they avoid it at all costs as it does cost; they succumb because they are experiencing discomfort and are sometimes in a lot of pain. So, they ask for the help of a dentist at great cost to remove the misery. A good dentist removes the distress quickly which begins the process of recovery. The client, after a time, realizes that the pain has gone and asks the question, "why am I still paying for a dentist?" So, the dentist is dispensed with and the client slowly reverts to eating sweets again. Months sometimes years later the pain returns and the client looks to a new dentist so as to avoid the chastising of the original dentist!'

The team nodded.

'What the clients need to do is develop their own in-house dentist to avoid pain, distress and cost. Given enough time I'd like to train you all.'

'So why don't they give you the time?' Mark asked.

'Well, it's a little embarrassing for the senior board to have such a quick turnaround when they were all in charge of creating the problem in the first place. That quick speed of improvement makes it even more galling to accept. It happens more times than you might think with interims.'

'Wow! Frank can you imagine what you could have achieved if you were here full time?' Mark smiled. This was a jibe for me leaving work on time!

We all laughed.

I drove out of the plant after saying goodbye to my team. Friendships were formed as a direct result of the ten months spent there. I smiled inside and beamed outside. An hour later I was sitting in the hotel bar with a large glass of chilled white wine pondering which holiday destination I fancied this time. The phone rang!

A number I didn't recognise.

Caller withheld!

'Hello. Frank Walsh.'

'Frank. I wondered if you're available for a chat? I have a customer who is tearing their hair out. I thought you could help?'

THE END

Note from Frank:

Thanks to everyone who bought the book, who made me JFDI, and I sincerely hope you get something from it and change the way you do things. Remember if you always do what you have always done, you will always get what you always got!

Please do get in touch if you need my service

Frank.walsh03@gmail.com

07544407209

Testimonials and notes:

The impact of Franks leadership style is best demonstrated by the progress achieved in the annual co-worker survey, Coveris Use the Dennison model for the survey and Louth achieved a year-on-year improvement of 25 points, the biggest single improvement of any Coveris site.

> Martin Davis. Chief Operating
> Officer. Coveris Division

* "The mentoring I personally received from Frank went far beyond what I anticipated. His counsel and practical wisdom on wide- ranging topics from the tools of lean management to branch network governance are experiences I will continue to hold with me."

> Matthew Kirby. Divisional Director –
> Glassolutions UK – Saint-Gobain

* "His mentoring of the GM and senior management team was essential to ensure profitability of the business…in that time Frank doubled output and reduced the backlog significantly…"

> Barry Coughlan. Executive Vice President,
> Deputy CEO – Rosti Group

* "I would recommend anyone needing to increase/ improve change current manufacturing processes to speak to Frank. He can and will make change happen."
    Michael Collett, CEO, Wila Lighting Group

* "A very astute people manager, he has always exceeded performance targets and has a proven reputation for getting results, particularly in a manufacturing environment."
        B. Hibbert, CEO, Polestar

* "His ability to deliver what he promises; he is very reliable in this regard. His skills are particularly well suited to an environment in need of dynamic change leadership."
        Patrick Pouliquen, Senior Vice President
        Air Climate Europe, Flakt Woods

* "Impressed by his vision for manufacturing, his engagement with team members, his awareness of customer needs, and most of all his drive and execution abilities ......He is very capable of developing and implementing an operations strategy, comfortable with hands on involvement, and has high energy levels and the capacity and confidence to drive change."
        Stephen Burton, Senior Vice President
        Human Resources, Flakt Woods

Supporting notes:

"The only way to become and stay lean is to produce lean managers. Every isolated effort will recede or fail unless companies learn to use the lean process as a way of developing individual problem –solvers with the ownership, initiative, and know how to solve problems, learn and ultimately coach new individuals in this discipline.
Source Jim Womack Lean Manager" 2010

So what's wrong with modern managers? The fraction of management time that actually results in improvements in the way these organisations create value must be pretty small, dwarfed by the amount of time they spend fighting fires. But, as on the shop floor, they are all good, well-intentioned people trapped in broken and dysfunctional management processes that drive them to do the wrong things.
Source Dan Jones AME May 2010

So, what is a 21st Century Manager? The above quotes I think sum it up for me. Having met both authors of the quotes, and been to many of their seminars it was very interesting to hear Jim Womack admit that after thirty years preaching the lean principles and philosophies, his conclusion is not a culture where individuals participate, but a participation of individuals creating the culture.

I studied many books and developed this simple test which summarizes what makes a 21st Century Manager.

Take this test to evaluate yourself as I have done; you will be surprised, and remember be honest with yourself on this as the only person your kidding is you!

Good luck!

So what type of manager are you?

Do you meet with all your direct reports every day to discuss the progress of their departments? YES or NO

Do you personally visit every customer with EVERY COMPLAINT?
YES/ NO _______________________

Do you believe first impressions matter?
YES/NO _______________________

Do you reward and recognize achievement with everyone?
YES/NO ________________

Does your organisation know (and you) that the purpose
is to create wealth?
YES/NO __________

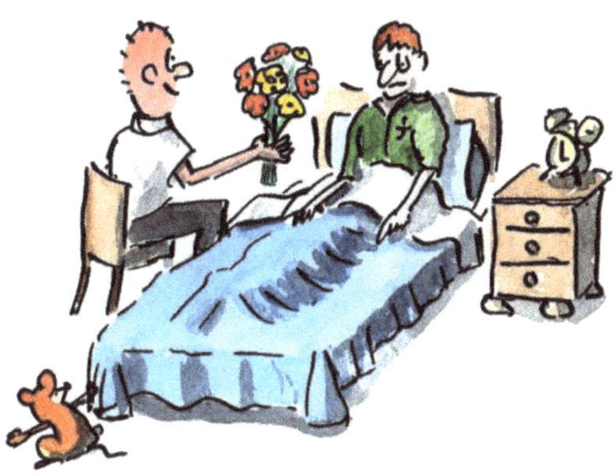

Do you care for every person within your organisation?
YES/NO _______________

Do you analyse each and every failure every day?
YES/NO _______________

Do you facilitate line management to your team members?
YES/NO _______________

Do you believe in solving problems, but not only by the few?
YES/NO _______________

Do you over complicate things?
YES/NO ___________________

Do you go and see each process and problem in each area,
every day?
YES/NO ___________________

Do your prioritize problems in each area and dedicate resources to resolve them every day?
YES/NO ______________

Do you have an efficient workforce trained to standards on each operation?
YES/NO ______________

Do you go and visit each process every hour every day?
YES/NO ___________________

Do you have teachers and mentors for each process?
YES/NO ___________________

Do you have meetings only after 2pm?
YES/NO _______________________

Are you a member of the laptop brigade? Stuck behind your laptop most of the day!
YES/NO _______________

So how did you do?
Write down your score total score here _______________________

So, which one of these types of manager best represents you and your style?

So, in your 21st Century Personal Improvement Plan, what would your prioritize of the 17?

So true leadership is summed up to me by observing a pack of wolves.

- **Three in front are old and sick, they walk in front to set the pace of the running group lest they get left behind**
- **The next five are the strongest and the best, they are tasked to protect the front side if there is an attack**
- **The pack in the middle are always protected from any attack**
- **The five behind them are also among the strongest and best: they are tasked to protect the back side if there is an attack**

- **The last one is the leader. He ensures that no one is left behind. He keeps the pack unified and on the same path. He is always ready to run in any direction to protect, and serves as the bodyguard to the entire group.**

Nelson Madela summed it up best:

"A leader is like a shepherd. He stays behind the flock, letting the nimblest go out ahead, whereupon the others follow, not realizing that all along they are being directed from behind."

9 781805 410966